Gloucestershire
MURDERS

Linda Stratmann

SUTTON PUBLISHING

First published in the United Kingdom in 2005 by
Sutton Publishing Limited · Phoenix Mill
Thrupp · Stroud · Gloucestershire · GL5 2BU

British Library Cataloguing in Publication Data
A catalogue record for this book is available from the British Library.

ISBN 0-7509-3950-8

To Gail

Typeset in 10/13pt Sabon
Typesetting and origination by
Sutton Publishing Limited.
Printed and bound in England by
J.H. Haynes & Co. Ltd, Sparkford.

CONTENTS

ACKNOWLEDGEMENTS

I would like to express my very grateful thanks to everyone who has assisted me with my research for this book, including all those who helped to make my time in Gloucestershire an enjoyable and fruitful one.

As always, the staff in my old haunts of the British Library, Colindale Newspaper Library, the Family Record Centre and the National Archives were immensely helpful.

Special thanks must go to: Robert and Elaine Jewell of St Augustine's Farm, Arlingham, for their enthusiasm and assistance with photographs; Keith and Ken Jones, West End Farm, Arlingham, for some delightful hospitality, and permission to photograph the scene of the crime; Sarah Manson of the Scribe's Alcove website www.scribes-alcove.co.uk for advice about the location of Catgrove Wood; and Mrs Frances Penney of Newent. Our serendipitous meeting with Mrs Penney in the graveyard of Newent church was a happy moment which led to a fascinating afternoon that I shall always remember. Her contribution to my research was of immense value.

INTRODUCTION

Gloucestershire is a county of enormous contrasts. Bisected by the great estuary of the Severn, it boasts rich farmlands, dramatic hills, peaceful villages of honey–coloured Cotswold stone, a legacy of silk and woollen mills, and the mines and quarries of the Forest of Dean. For many years Bristol was a part of the county, and its thriving trade and expanding population made it the second city in England.

Murder, too, can come in many guises: a moment of passion; a carefully executed plot; a pitched affray at the dead of night; and sometimes a murder that may have been no murder at all. Not all of the cases in this book have been solved, and many leave us with fascinating questions to engage our minds long after we first encounter them.

In my research I have made extensive use of contemporary documents, including trial transcripts, newspapers, the records of Assizes, the Metropolitan Police and Director of Public Prosecutions held in the National Archives, and family history archives. I especially appreciate the invaluable local knowledge provided by the friendly and welcoming people of Gloucestershire.

1
THE CAMPDEN WONDER

Chipping Campden, 1660–2

Chipping Campden is a small market town built of honey-coloured stone, lying on the edge of the Cotswold Hills. Many of its buildings date back to the fourteenth century, when the town first became of note through its connection with the wool trade. By the seventeenth century that trade was in decline, and the town settled into a more peaceful mode of life, only to be disturbed by a series of events at once dramatic, tragic and inexplicable.

The Manor of Campden was purchased in 1609 by Baptist Hicks, a Gloucestershire man who had amassed a great fortune through trade. A generous man, he built a row of substantial almshouses in 1612 and a market house in 1627. In 1613 he built himself a noble house near the church, the outside of which was reputed to have cost him £29,000, a sum equivalent to about £3.5 million today. There he ordered lights to be set up on dark nights for the benefit of travellers. In 1628 he was created Viscount Campden of Campden, but having no son to inherit his fortune and title, he procured a special licence by which all his honours and titles passed on his death in 1629 to the Noel family, Sir Edward Noel being the husband of his eldest daughter, Juliana. Edward Noel died in 1643 and the title passed to his son, Baptist Noel. The Hicks and Noel families were ardent Royalists during the Civil War, and the manor house served as a garrison for the King's men. When they were forced to

Memorial to Lord Edward and Lady Juliana Noel, St James's Church, Chipping Campden. (Author's collection)

quit it, however, they were afraid that it would fall into the hands of the Parliamentarians, and rather than have this happen the house was deliberately burned to the ground. Only some outlying buildings survived, including the gateway, the stables, which were later converted into accommodation for Lady Juliana, and the East Banqueting Pavilion.

It is probable that in 1660, when the extraordinary events that came to be known as the Campden Wonder started to unfold, Lady Juliana, who was then about 74 years of age, was not living in Campden but at the Noel family estates in Rutland. She still retained an interest in the Campden estate and employed a trusted steward, William Harrison, to collect the rents. In 1660 Harrison was about 70 years of age, and he had served the Noel family for fifty years. It is thought that he was then living in one of the remaining outbuildings of the estate, quite probably the East Banqueting Pavilion. Harrison, a respected man in the community, was a feoffee – a governor – of the Chipping Campden Grammar School, the accounts of which provide samples of his signature. Another feoffee was local magistrate Sir Thomas Overbury, whose uncle and namesake had come to an unfortunate end in the Tower of London in 1613. It is to Overbury's account of the Campden Wonder, written many years after the events, that we are chiefly indebted for the story.

In 1660 the legal and political affairs of the country were in a state of turmoil. Richard Cromwell had ceased to act as Lord Protector in May 1659, and the judges he had appointed were no longer in office. New judges had been appointed by the Long Parliament, but after this was dissolved in March 1660 it was uncertain whether their decisions remained valid. Charles II was not declared lawful king until 8 May, and even after that the restoration of the monarchy was still in doubt until Charles arrived in London three weeks later. Although the King's new parliament promised to pass an Act of Indemnity and Oblivion, pardoning offences committed during the conflict (apart, of course, from those connected with his father's death), it was by no means certain that this would happen, and the matter was hotly debated for the next three months.

On the afternoon of Thursday 16 August 1660 William Harrison set out to walk from Campden to the village of Charringworth 2 miles away to collect the rents. He first collected £23 from Edward Plaisterer, then called at the house of William Curtis, but Curtis was out, and Harrison did not wait for him. Turning homewards, he stopped at the village of Ebrington, which was mid-way between Charringworth and Campden, where he paid a brief visit to the home of one of the villagers, called Daniel. After that he disappeared. Mrs Harrison, waiting at home for her husband's arrival, began to worry about him as the evening wore on, and between 8 and 9 p.m. sent her servant, John Perry, to look for his master. Neither man returned that night.

At the time of these events John Perry was about 25 years old and had probably served the Harrison family since boyhood. His mother, Joan, had been widowed about three years previously. John had one surviving brother, Richard, and several sisters. Richard, seven years John's senior, had effectively been head of

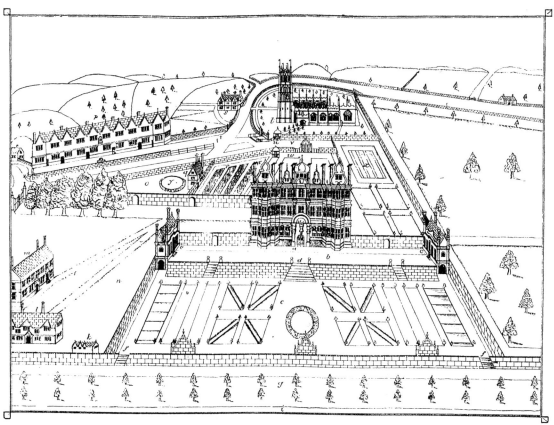

BIRDSEYE VIEW OF CAMPDEN HOUSE, BURNT DOWN IN THE YEAR OF NASEBY, 1645 (from an old drawing).

References—*a* The house. *b* The terrass walk. *c* The banquiting house. *d* The garden staires. *e* The great garden. *f* The orchart staires.
g The great orchart. *i* The long canal. *k* The coach-house. *l* The brew-house. *m* The stables. *n* The stable court. *o* The henn yard.
p The hospital. *q* The laundry. *r* The bleach garden. *s* The parsonage house. *t* The church. *u* The porter's lodge. *v* The outward
court. *w* The great court. *x* The garden court. *y* The pond.

Campden House and Estate before 1645, from a contemporary drawing. (British Library)

the family since his father's death and was married with children, whereas John
was single.

Early on the morning of 17 August Edward, William Harrison's son, went out to
trace his father's footsteps and on the way to Charringworth encountered John
Perry, who informed him that his master was not there. The two men went to
Ebrington, where they spoke to Daniel. Half a mile away was the village of
Paxford, where they made enquiries, but Harrison had not been seen there. The
trail had gone cold. Turning their steps towards Campden again, the men must have
anxiously questioned everyone they met on the way, and were told of a hat, collar
band and comb that had been found in the road between Campden and Ebrington
by a poor woman who had gone to glean in a field. They at once went to look for
the woman and, finding her, were able to confirm that the items were the property
of William Harrison. Disturbingly, they had been much hacked and cut about, and
there was blood on the collar. Edward now felt sure that his father had been

attacked and murdered, probably by robbers, and asked the woman to show them where she had found the items. She led them down the roadway near a bank of gorse bushes. A search was made, but there was no trace of the missing man.

Suspicion naturally fell on John Perry, who had thus far failed to explain why he had stayed out all night. On the following day he was examined before a Justice of the Peace, who was not named in Overbury's pamphlet but may have been Overbury himself, which would account for his detailed knowledge of the case. Perry said that having travelled a land's length (a furlong, or 201m) on his way to Charringworth, he had met William Reed of Campden, and told him of his errand. He told Reed that he was afraid, as it was growing dark, and thought he would return, fetch his young master's horse (presumably Edward's) and come back. The two men walked to Harrison's court gate (probably the gate leading to the courtyard of the old Campden House). There the two men parted, Reed going his own way, but Perry, for reasons he never explained, did not go to get the horse, but stayed where he was. A man called Pearce next happened by and Perry walked with him into the fields for a 'bow's shot' (about 200 yards) before returning with him to his master's gate, where they parted. By now, Perry's wanderings back and forth and standing around had occupied two hours, during which Mrs Harrison no doubt thought he was searching for her husband. Perry then went into his master's hen-roost and lay there for an hour, without sleeping. When the church clock struck midnight he got up and went towards Charring-worth. Then, he said, a great mist arose and he lost his way, so he spent the rest of the night lying under a hedge. At daybreak he continued his journey to Charringworth, where he spoke to Edward Plaisterer and William Curtis. By now it was 5 a.m., and the sun was rising, so Perry set out for home, meeting up with Edward Harrison on the way.

At first glance Perry's tale looks highly suspicious; however, all the four men he mentioned supported what he had said as regards themselves. The Justice asked him how come he was so bold as to go to Charringworth at midnight when he had been afraid to go there at nine? Perry replied that he was afraid at nine because it was dark, whereas at midnight there was a moon. Records show that moonrise that night was at about 10.30 p.m., so we can assume that at midnight the moon was well risen and bright. The Justice also asked him why, having twice returned home, did he not think to go into the house to see if his master had returned while he was out? Perry said that he knew his master was not home as there was a light in his chamber window which never used to be there so late when he was at home. It is possible that Mrs Harrison had placed a light in the window to help light her husband home. Harrison usually retired to bed early, so had he been home the light would have been out. It does seem strange that Perry, who was born and bred in Chipping Campden, managed to lose his way, even in the mist, but he was clearly unwilling to go about when he could not see his way. All his odd behaviour can be accounted for by fear of the dark. His waiting around was for enough moonlight to travel by, and he at once attached himself nervously to any passer-by who would keep him company.

Perry was kept in custody pending further enquiries. He remained in Campden either at the inn or in the common prison from Saturday 18 August to the following Friday. During this time the same Justice questioned him again, but his story remained the same. It was later rumoured that, being often pressed to tell all he knew, he had satisfied his listeners with more than one story, telling some that his master had been killed by a tinker, others that a gentleman's servant of the neighbourhood had robbed and killed him, and still others that he had been killed and his body placed in a bean-rick. The bean-rick was duly searched but nothing was found.

Eventually, Perry stated that if he could speak to the Justice again he would tell him something that he would say to no one else. On Friday 24 August he was brought before the Justice and said that his master had been murdered, but not by him. The murderers, he said, were his own mother and brother. The Justice, shocked at this unexpected revelation, quite rightly cautioned him, saying he feared that John might be the guilty one, and asked him not to draw more innocent blood on his head, for the charge might well cost his mother and brother their lives. Perry stuck to his story. He said that ever since he had been in service with Mr Harrison, his mother and brother had pestered him to tell them when his master went to collect the rents so they could waylay and rob him.

John then launched into a detailed description of the murder of William Harrison. He said that on the morning of Thursday 16 August he had gone into town on an errand. There he met his brother, Richard, in the street and set matters in motion by telling him where Harrison was going that day. That evening, after being sent out to look for his master, he had met Richard again by Harrison's gate, and they walked together to the churchyard. There they had parted, John taking the footpath across the churchyard and Richard keeping to the main road around the church. Why they should have parted at this point John never explained, but a search for Harrison seems the most likely motive. In the highway beyond the church the brothers met up again, and walked to the gate a bow's shot from the church that led into ground belonging to Lady Campden called the Conygree. For anyone who held a key to the gate, which his master did, it was the quickest way to Harrison's house. John said he had seen someone, who he assumed was his master, go into the Conygree and told Richard that if he followed he would have the money. Declining to take part in the crime himself, he went for a walk in the fields. After a while he followed his brother into the Conygree, and there found his master lying on the ground, Richard standing over him and their mother standing nearby. 'Ah, rogues, will you kill me?' Harrison had exclaimed. John told his brother that he hoped he would not kill his master, but Richard said, 'Peace, peace, you're a fool', and strangled Harrison. He then took a bag of money from Harrison's pocket and threw it into his mother's lap. John and Richard carried the body from the Conygree to the adjoining garden, where they discussed what to do with it. They decided to throw it into the 'great sink' (probably a cesspool) by Wallington's Mill behind the garden. Richard and his mother sent John to the court next to the house to listen if anyone was

The East Banqueting Pavilion, Chipping Campden. (Author's collection)

stirring, but he chose not to return to them, going instead to the court gate where he encountered John Pearce, as mentioned in his original statement. John Perry had with him his master's hat, band and comb; later, after giving them some cuts with his knife, he threw them on the highway, where the poor woman found them, so as to make people think his master had been robbed there.

The strange thing about Perry's tale which no one seems to have commented on at the time was that Harrison was said to have returned home well after Perry was sent to search for him, in other words when he had already been missing long enough for his wife to be worried.

On hearing this story the Justice had no option but to give orders for the arrest of Joan and Richard Perry, and for the sink to be dragged for the body. No trace of Harrison could be found, however, either there or in the fish ponds, or in the ruins of Old Campden House, all of which were thoroughly searched.

On Saturday 25 August all three Perrys were brought before the Justice, where Richard and Joan indignantly denied all the charges. Richard agreed that he had met his brother in town on the Thursday in question, but that their conversation was nothing to do with Harrison's going to Charringworth. He and his mother now rounded on John, saying he was a villain to tell such lies, but John stuck to his story.

As the three prisoners were returning from the Justice's house to Campden, Richard pulled a cloth from his pocket and with it came a ball of inkle, a kind of linen tape. One of the guards picked it up and Richard explained that it was a hair-lace belonging to his wife. Noticing that the length of inkle had a slip knot in it, the guard showed it to John and asked whether he knew it. John shook his head sorrowfully and said that he did, for that was the string his brother had used to strangle his master.

The next day being Sunday, the Minister of Campden (probably the Revd William Bartholemew) asked to speak to the prisoners, and they were brought to the church. On the way they passed Richard's house, and two of his children went out to meet him. He took the smaller in his arms and led the other by the hand. Suddenly, both started to bleed at the nose, an event which was seen as ominous.

The Justice, having thought over the statements made by John Perry, now recalled some unusual events in the recent past which he thought might be related to Harrison's disappearance. In the previous year Harrison's house had been burgled, between eleven and twelve noon, on Campden market day when all the family was out. They had returned home to find leaning against the wall a ladder leading to a second-storey window. The window had been barred with iron, but the bar had been wrenched off with a ploughshare, which was later found in the room. A sum of £140 was missing. The culprits were never found.

More recently, only a few weeks before Harrison's disappearance, John Perry had been heard making a huge outcry in the garden. He had come running out in a great state of alarm with a sheep-pick (a pitchfork) in his hand, saying he had been set upon by two men in white with naked swords, and he had defended himself with the sheep-pick. The handle of the implement was cut in two or three places and a key in his pocket was also cut, which he said had been done with their swords. He himself seemed to be uninjured.

John Perry was closely questioned about these two incidents and said that it was his brother who had committed the burglary. He said he had not been there at the time but he had told his brother where the money was kept and where he might find a ladder. Richard had afterwards told him he had buried the money in the garden. The attack on himself he confessed to being a fiction, to make people think that rogues haunted the place, so that when his master was burgled it would be thought they had done it. The Justice ordered a search to be made for the money, but nothing was found.

While the prisoners awaited trial an event happened that was to have an important effect on the outcome of their case. On 29 August 1660 the Act of Indemnity and Oblivion was finally passed. At the assizes in September Joan, John and Richard had two indictments found against them; one was for the burglary and the other for the murder of William Harrison. The judge of the assizes, who is generally thought to have been Sir Christopher Turnor, an eminent and highly respected man, refused to try the Perrys on the second count, as no body had been found, but they were then tried for the burglary. All three initially pleaded not guilty, but at this some whispering was heard behind them; after some consultation they changed their plea to guilty but begged the benefit of the pardon conferred by the Act of Indemnity and Oblivion, which applied to the 1659 burglary, although it could not apply to the more recent charge. It is very probable that they had been advised by their lawyers to make this plea in order to save the time of the court. It was, as it turned out, a fatally bad piece of advice. All three were granted a pardon under the new Act, although after the trial they continued to deny any guilt in or knowledge of the burglary. In the meantime, John Perry continued to say that his mother and brother had murdered Harrison. He also accused them of trying to poison him while he was in the jail, so that he dared not eat and drink with them.

The Perrys remained in jail until the next assizes the following spring, when the murder indictment was placed before a different judge, Sir Robert Hyde, who was known for his severity. All three pleaded not guilty to the murder, and John retracted his accusation, saying that when he made it he was mad and had not known what he was saying. Since none of John's several accounts of his master's death or the details he had given of the burglary had been supported by any evidence, there were good grounds for belief that nothing he said should be given any credence. Richard and Joan said they knew nothing of what had happened to William Harrison, and Richard pointed out that John had accused others, too, though no names were placed before the court. Unfortunately, all three were now considered to be proven criminals after pleading guilty to robbery, and Hyde was not so particular about the fact that no body had been found. The Perrys were found guilty of the murder of William Harrison and sentenced to hang.

A few days later all three were brought to the top of Broadway Hill near Campden, where a gibbet had been erected. Edward Harrison stood at the foot of the ladder to observe the executions. As it was rumoured that Joan was a witch and that her sons would be unable to confess while she was alive, she was executed first. With his mother's body dangling from the gibbet, Richard was next to ascend the ladder. As he did so, he professed his innocence and said that he knew nothing of what had become of Mr Harrison. In his final words he beseeched John for the satisfaction of the whole world and his own conscience to declare what he knew. John, with a dogged and surly manner, told the watching crowds that he wasn't obliged to confess to them. Richard was hanged, and as John prepared for death there must have been some anticipation that he would at last resolve the mystery. Disappointingly, he said that he knew nothing about his master's death, or what had become of him, though he hinted that they might possibly hear something in years to come. He died without a confession. The bodies of Joan and Richard were later taken down and buried near the place of execution, but John's was left to hang in chains.

Two years passed, and the body of John Perry had rotted where it hung, when William Harrison returned to Chipping Campden. The reaction of his family and friends has not been recorded, though it is easy to imagine delight and amazement at his appearance being mingled with sickening guilt. He resumed his previous

Broadway Tower, built in 1799 on the site of the execution of the Perrys. (Author's collection)

duties, including the governorship of the school, where a comparison of his signatures with the accounts before and after the incident can leave no doubt that this was indeed William Harrison. He claimed in a letter to Sir Thomas Overbury to have been attacked by strangers, stabbed in the side and thigh with a sword, and abducted. Money had been stuffed in his pockets, and he had been carried on horseback to Deal on the Kent coast, where he had been placed on board a ship bound for Turkey. He was there sold for £7 as a slave to an elderly physician and remained there until his master's death almost two years later. He then found a ship going to London and returned home.

The story is ridiculous on several counts. Who would abduct a man of 70 in order to transport him overseas and sell him as a slave for a few pounds? Why was he wounded, requiring his captors to spend much time and trouble nursing him back to health? Why was money stuffed in his pockets? How was he transported on horseback from Gloucestershire to Kent without anyone noticing? An account of the incident and a ballad, both published in 1662 by Charles Tyus, who was unwilling to admit that three innocent people had been executed, stated that Harrison had indeed been attacked and robbed by the Perrys, who flung him into a pit, but once he recovered his senses, Joan Perry's witchcraft had instantly transported him from the spot. Even Harrison had never suggested that the Perrys had anything to do with his missing two years.

The Campden Wonder leaves us with two great mysteries – what happened to William Harrison, and how do we explain John Perry's behaviour?

The most probable reason for William Harrison's disappearance was that he deliberately faked his own death after embezzling funds belonging to Lady Campden, something which could have gone on for many years. The restoration of the monarchy, the return to order and the appointment of king's judges could well have made him fear discovery. It is unlikely that he even left the country, but took with him such funds as he had in order to make a new life. He may never have intended to return to Chipping Campden, but was forced to when his money ran out. Whether he knew anything of the fate of the Perrys, it is impossible to say.

Did Mrs Harrison know her husband's secret? Anthony Wood, an Oxford antiquary and contemporary of Overbury, wrote some notes on a copy of Overbury's account held in the Bodleian Library, in which he claimed that after Harrison's return his wife, 'being a snotty covetuous [sic] Presbyterian', hanged herself. Another edition of Overbury's pamphlet in the Bodleian has a letter attached, dated 1780, from a Charringworth man, Mr Barnsley, to antiquary John Gough, stating that after Harrison's return Mrs Harrison hanged herself, and a letter was later found in her effects written by her husband before the execution of the Perrys. The inference is that Mrs Harrison stayed silent to protect her husband, and knowingly allowed three innocent people, all of whom she must have known, to go to their deaths. On her husband's return guilt, and maybe local gossip, drove her to suicide. It is impossible to confirm whether these stories are true or just inventions intended to add drama to an already tragic tale. Since Mrs Harrison's Christian name is unknown and the surname was a common one in the area, it is not possible to discover her date of death. It has also been suggested that Edward Harrison was in some way involved, wanting to remove his father so he could gain the stewardship, which he later did, but there is no evidence for this.

Wood, who was perhaps repeating local rumours, added a fanciful tale about a gentlewoman who ordered Joan's body to be dug up, so she could learn more about witchcraft. When her horse shied away from the body she struck her head on John's dangling feet and fell into the grave. Wood also alleged that on Harrison's return a messenger brought the news to Sir Robert Hyde, the judge at the Perrys' murder trial, who accused him of lying and had him flung in prison. Whether this is true or not, it certainly says something about opinions of Hyde's administration of justice.

It is too easy to suggest that Perry was mentally subnormal or simply insane. One popular theory is that he was schizophrenic and subject to delusions; however, he had worked for Harrison for some time, was trusted enough to be sent out to find him, and his evidence is detailed and coherently given. Had he been 'simple-minded' or obviously delusional, this would have been well known locally and would probably have emerged at the questioning. That said, there is

Signatures of William Harrison. From top to bottom, 9 April 1657, 5 April 1660 and 15 October 1663. (Chipping Grammar School Accounts Book)

some evidence of a personality disorder, which took the form of attention-seeking behaviour arising out of a feeling of inadequacy. Nothing is known of such behaviour in his early life, but there are some very striking incidents that suggest Perry was adept at using events to place himself at the centre of attention, either in a heroic role or as a victim.

The first such incident is the burglary at Harrison's house. Perry said nothing about this at the time, but later he accused his brother of the crime and claimed he knew where the money was hidden. One question that should be asked is whether this robbery ever actually occurred. It is supposed to have taken place in broad daylight when the Harrison family was away from home. It would have been simple for Harrison to hide the funds where he could later retrieve them, place a ladder at the window, wrench off the iron bar and claim that he had been robbed.

The second such event is the supposed attack on Perry by the armed men. Such accusations are common among those who seek attention. The 'ball of inkle' incident also shows that he was quick-witted enough immediately to turn an unexpected incident to his own account.

It has been suggested that Perry suffered from the disorder that leads people to confess to high-profile crimes but, looking at his statement in detail, we can see that he never actually confessed to the murder. He confessed only to telling his brother where he might find Harrison and also to placing the hat, comb and band on the road. It is very possible that John Perry was under the impression that by giving these details he would find himself not in the dock but in the witness box, with a starring role in the trial, exempt from prosecution, by turning 'King's evidence'. When he was accused of murder he retracted his confession and said that he must have been mad when he made his original statement – not what one might expect of someone who was delusional, who would have stuck to the story to the end.

Perry's behaviour reveals not only a wish to draw attention to himself but also a deep, festering resentment of his mother and brother. Whether this was present in his early years we do not know, but matters may have arisen or been exacerbated on his father's death, when his brother – a more successful man, married with a family and more respected in Campden than John, who remained a lowly servant – was accepted as head of the family. It may have been, or seemed to John, that Richard was his mother's favourite. By accusing them both of crimes, John not only achieved the celebrity he craved but also removed the two people he felt had consigned him to an inferior role. The conclusion emerges that John Perry, while not emotionally normal, was nonetheless sane, and when he accused his mother and brother of murder he acted deliberately, knowing exactly what he was doing. He was not expecting the ploy to backfire on him, with fatal consequences, and by the time he retracted his story it was too late.

Did John Perry know about Harrison's disappearance or even connive at it, placing the hat, comb and band in the road for him? This seems unlikely. Harrison was fully capable of planting the items himself on the afternoon of his disappearance, and if Perry had really known all about it, he would hardly have gone to his death to preserve Harrison's secret. Perry's hints of hidden information shortly before he was hanged were just his last stab at celebrity.

William Harrison's signature continued to appear in the school registers until 1672, in which year it is probable that he died, taking his secrets to the grave.

2
LEGACY OF DEATH

River Severn, 1741

In the eighteenth century, Bristol, a centre of trade since ancient times, was enjoying a golden age of commerce. Standing in the centre of coal-producing country, it was also close to the rich farmlands of Wales, Gloucestershire, Somerset and Wiltshire. Second only to London in size and importance, it was in a key location for transatlantic shipping and the Irish ports, while the deep, navigable waters of the Avon had been made accessible to major vessels as far as Bath. Ships passing through the Bristol Channel could find safe and sheltered anchorage at roadsteads such as Kingroad, where they could wait for a favourable tide. In the heart of Bristol was the great Quay, known as the Gibb, a mile-long wharf of hewn stone.

Broad Quay Bristol, early eighteenth century. (Contemporary painting/British Library)

On the afternoon of Sunday 19 January 1741 (usually given as 1740 in contemporary documents, since under the Julian calendar – which Britain used until September 1752, when it adopted the Gregorian – New Year's Day was 25 March), there was a great commotion in the streets of Bristol. Passers-by began to follow a knot of men who were hurrying down the Rope-walk to where a barge was waiting near the King's Head public house, and such was the noise that drinkers emerged from the tavern to see what was going on. They saw a well-dressed man of about 60 being half dragged and half carried along the street by a gang of ruffianly looking sailors, their captain urging them on. The man was crying out for help, saying he was about to be murdered, but when people approached the sailors threatened them with truncheons and told them to keep away, while their captain claimed that the man was a murderer being taken for trial. As he was forced on to the barge, the man made one more appeal to the crowds, shouting out that his name was Sir John Dineley Goodere and someone should go and tell his solicitor, Mr Jarrit Smith, that he was going to be murdered. The captain put a hand over Goodere's mouth and ordered his men to row. What none of the onlookers knew was that the captain was Sir John's younger brother.

Sir John's family had had a troubled history. Marriage between the Dineleys and Gooderes had brought a large estate to Sir John's father, all of which was settled on the eldest son, Edward. The two younger sons – John, who was born in about 1680, and Samuel, born in 1687 – were sent to sea. When Edward was killed in a duel John suddenly found himself the heir, and he was summoned home in 1709 to be groomed for his new responsibilities.

Sir John's new-found status provoked a deep and lasting resentment in his brother, who had been wild and lawless from his youth. While at school Samuel had led a group of companions to rob his grandfather's house and had even threatened his own mother with a pistol. He had once written to his father demanding money, saying that he would lie in wait for him and shoot him if he did not comply. It must have been a relief when he was at sea. Samuel did not have a successful career. In 1719 he was a lieutenant, and during an action off St Sebastian, Spain, had been sent to lead an attack on a neighbouring island. He returned having failed to carry out his orders and was court-martialled and dismissed. After a review in 1720 he was placed on half pay. Samuel went to live with his father, and after the death of his first wife, Eleanor, he married a widow, Elizabeth Watts of Monmouthshire, who bore him twin sons, Edward and John, in 1729. Samuel became involved in politics and through his family connections (his father had been MP for both Evesham and Herefordshire) was able to obtain favours that elevated him to a captaincy. In 1733 he was reinstated to full pay. In that year both brothers stood for the office of Mayor in Evesham, and both were elected. When Sir John arrived at church to be enthroned Samuel could not bear to see his brother in the mayor's seat, so he had his servants remove him to a humbler place and took the seat himself. Sir John quietly conceded, as it was not a place for wrangling.

When their father died in 1739 Samuel at once hurried to the estate at
Burhope, Hereford, and once there demanded that Sir John leave the house,
claiming that the estate was his by virtue of a lease granted before their father's
death. Sir John produced the will, showing that the estate was his for life, only
going to Samuel after his death. Samuel brushed this aside, saying that his deed
had priority. Asked to produce this document, however, he could not. His manner
now became belligerent. If Sir John did not quit the house immediately, he said,
he would set upon him six bulldogs he had at the door and make him repent his
refusal. The bulldogs turned out to be six sturdy seamen, who strode in and were
about to attack Sir John when Elizabeth fell at her husband's feet and begged him
not to carry out his threats. The brief pause gave Sir John just enough time to act
– he ran upstairs and found a blunderbuss. But there was a snag – there was no
powder or shot. Hoping that Samuel would not realise this, he threatened his
brother and his men with the unloaded firearm, and ordered them to leave. To his
great relief the bluff worked, and they departed. There was now a state of
undisguised antagonism between the two brothers, although friends often tried –
and failed – to get them to settle their differences. Samuel still had his eye on his
brother's estate, but Sir John made a will leaving everything to his sister's
descendants, the Foote family, which Samuel knew he would have to try to
overturn.

In 1716 Sir John had married Mary Lawford of Stapleton, near Bristol, who
brought with her a considerable property. There were two sons from the
marriage: John, who died before 1730, and Edward, whose riotous behaviour
caused a falling-out between father and son. Sir John later expressed doubts that
the boy was his and had him apprenticed to a saddler. Sir John treated his wife
with callous cruelty, keeping her short of necessities and subjecting her to both
verbal and physical abuse. He once dragged her out of bed and had her chained
in a garret, where he left her all night. In the winter of 1730 he turned her out of
the house into the snowy street at midnight. Not dressed for the cold, she was
obliged to take refuge with a neighbour. Believing her life to be in danger, she
eventually left her husband, and he at once accused her of desertion. Even living
apart he would not let her alone. One evening she was travelling by coach when
he rode up and fired his pistols at her through the window. Fortunately it was
dark and he missed. Later, when she lay ill in bed in lodgings, he tried to force his
way into her room and demanded that her landlord evict her. At another inn he
both threatened to kill her and assaulted her. He accused his wife of adultery with
Sir Robert Jason, Baronet, and, when the matter came to court bribed a witness
to testify in his favour. Found guilty of conspiracy, Mary Goodere was jailed for
twelve months. It was in 1739, while she lay in prison, that her only surviving
son, Edward, became dangerously ill.

Edward lay dying of consumption, destitute in an alehouse, knowing that if he
recovered he would be sent to jail for debt. A substantial estate had been entailed
upon him, and he had made a will leaving everything to his mother, ordering that
his father should have no power to interfere with her discretion to dispose of the

property. It suited Samuel to see the property pass to Mary, as he had sided with her against his brother. On his deathbed, however, Edward proposed to transfer the property to his father on consideration of an annuity and settlement of his debts. Edward was taken to an attorney's house in Fetter Lane, London, and there the necessary documents were signed. He died two days later. When Samuel heard about this he was determined to prove that there had been a fraud and accused his brother of completing the signature himself, with the pen in the grasp of his dead son's hand. Samuel brought a legal action, but even after he bribed witnesses to give evidence in his favour it failed.

Captain Samuel Goodere. (Contemporary woodcut/British Library)

When Sir John succeeded to his father's estates in 1739 he determined to marry again and produce an heir, so he brought before the House of Lords a bill for divorce against Mary. Samuel assisted her in opposing the bill, with the result that the Lords refused to grant the divorce and awarded Mary her costs. In the following year Samuel Goodere was made master of a man-of-war, the *Ruby*. He still hoped to find some means of appropriating the family estates, but matters were exacerbated by Sir John's arranging to borrow money against his property thus reducing the value of what Samuel thought should be his. In January 1741 the *Ruby* was lying at Kingroad, but the vessels it was due to escort would not be ready for a week: this delay gave Samuel the opportunity to put into action a plan to dispose of his brother.

Through a mutual friend, Thomas Chamberlayne, he approached Jarrit Smith, his brother's solicitor, whose house was on College Green between St Augustine's Church and the Cathedral, and asked him to arrange a meeting at his home to bring about a reconciliation. Smith – a respected man in the city who later became MP for Bristol and a baronet – must have been both pleased and flattered. He discussed the idea with Sir John, who doubted that a meeting would serve any purpose but, out of his friendship with and regard for Smith, agreed. The date set was Tuesday 13 January. On the Monday Samuel, dressed in a fine scarlet cloak with his sword at his side, arrived at the White Hart Inn, College Green, which stood opposite Smith's house. He was accompanied by 21-year-old Matthew Mahony. Born in Ennis, Ireland, Mahony was destined to be a farmer, but he had a roving inclination and had gone to sea. According to a contemporary, 'while a boy he was always reckoned of a rough disposition, and cruel ill-natured temper, and ready for any mischief'. This suited his captain, who 'found him to be bold and daring, and made him his confidant on several occasions'. Mahony's light, active build, 'proof against toil and fatigue', made him an ideal runner, scampering about quickly on his master's business. Before he departed Samuel hired the Inn's upper room over the porch for the purpose of breakfasting the following morning. When he returned on the Tuesday he was wearing a drab coat with the cape buttoned close under his hat, so well disguised that the landlord, Mr Hobbs, did not at first know it was the same gentleman as before. Mahony arrived, as did seven or eight other men, and Samuel ordered food and drink for them. Hobbs noticed that, as they waited, the men constantly looked out of the door or window at Jarrit Smith's house. Samuel breakfasted in the room above, and Mahony was seen frequently darting up and down the stairs to report on events below.

When Sir John arrived at Jarrit Smith's house, however, he told Smith he wanted to postpone the meeting. He said his head was bad and he needed to go to Bath for treatment, but promised to be back the following Sunday. Sir John's servant arrived with the horses; and from across the road, the watchers saw that both men were carrying pistols. Samuel ordered his men to follow them to see where they went, but not to touch them.

When Samuel was advised of the postponement he hired the same room at the White Hart for the following Sunday. On that day Samuel's men returned, together

THE FRATRICIDE,

OR

THE MURDERER'S GIBBET;

BEING PART THE SECOND OF THE

Right Tragical Hystorie of Sir John D. Goodere, Bart.

The White Hart Inn, c. 1741. (Contemporary engraving/British Library)

with a number of privateers he had hired, and a careful watch was kept as before. The landlord noticed their unusual behaviour but seems not to have suspected that anything criminal was intended – or perhaps he preferred not to know.

The two brothers finally met at Smith's house at 3 p.m. Their encounter was cordial – they embraced, and Samuel drank to Sir John's health, his brother (as was his habit) drinking only water. After about half an hour Sir John departed, and as he walked down the hill a well-satisfied Jarrit Smith, viewing his friend's receding

The abduction of Sir John Dineley Goodere.
(Contemporary engraving/
British Library)

figure, said to Samuel, 'I think I have done great things for you.' To his surprise, Samuel exclaimed, 'By God this won't do!' and strode down the hill after his brother. Smith did not see what happened next. Samuel's men quickly ran out of the White Hart and, catching up with Sir John, asked him to go with them, as a gentleman wanted to speak to him. No gentleman appearing, Sir John soon became suspicious, and they began forcibly to haul him along the street, over St Augustine's Butts, along the Rope-walk and to Hot-well, near to which the barge lay, Samuel encouraging them to hurry along.

As the barge pulled away Sir John said, 'I know you mean to murder me this night, and therefore you may as well do it now.' Samuel denied any such intention, saying he only wanted to stop him spending the estate, yet he still urged his brother to make his peace with God. 'Have you not given the rogues of lawyers money enough already?' he said. 'Do you want to give them more? I will take care that they shall never have any more of you; now I'll take care of you.' As the oars splashed, the two brothers continued to bicker. When the barge briefly put in to shore to drop off the team of privateers Samuel had hired, Sir John saw a man he recognised and cried out to him, but a cloak was thrown over him, muffling his words.

Jarrit Smith went out soon after the meeting and did not return home until 5 p.m. He was approached by a soldier who told him that while he had been drinking at the King's Head alehouse at the Lime-kiln he had seen Sir John being forced on to the barge, and he had cried out that Jarrit Smith should be told. Smith knew that Sir John had been going in the direction of his lodgings, so he hurried there and discovered that his friend had not been seen since he went out for the meeting. This was the moment when Jarrit Smith, who knew better than any man about the past enmity between the brothers, should have taken action. Instead, he seems to have done nothing about it until the following morning, a delay that was literally fatal.

The barge reached the *Ruby* at 7 p.m. Samuel had already had the purser's cabin prepared for a visitor, having primed his men to expect a madman to be brought on board for treatment. Sir John was forced into the cabin, where Samuel chatted to him and offered him rum, but Sir John tetchily insisted he had not touched alcohol in two years. Samuel then called for Daniel Weller, the ship's carpenter, to put two strong bolts on the cabin door. As this was being done Sir John told Weller that his brother had brought him there to murder him, but Weller reassured him it was only to look after him. James Dudgeon, the surgeon's mate, was told that Sir John was 'a crazy old man' and was asked to examine him. He took the patient's pulse and asked how he was. Sir John complained of a bad cold and a headache, as well as pain from his earlier rough usage. This formality over, the cabin door was locked and Samuel told one of his men, Duncan Buchanan, to stand sentry outside with a cutlass.

The purser's cabin was separated only by a thin wall from the one next to it, which was occupied by Edward Jones, the ship's cooper, and his wife. He heard Sir John pray to God to be his comforter, as he knew he was going to be murdered, but as Jones had already been told that the man was crazy, he did not attach any importance to this. The couple went to bed at 8 p.m. Some time later Jones heard the man knock and call out that he wanted to relieve himself. Eventually Mahony brought him a bucket. The two men talked, and Sir John told Mahony of his exploits at sea. Sir John was left alone again, and soon all was quiet. Jones and his wife went to sleep.

Late that night, Samuel called Mahony to his cabin and told him he must murder his brother, who was mad and must not live till four o'clock in the morning. If there had been any hesitation on Mahony's part it was removed by a liberal supply of rum and the promise of money. Mahony said he couldn't do it alone, so Samuel said they must get another man to help. Elisha Cole was the man suggested, but he was drunk. Their second choice was Charles White, aged 36, a 'stout lusty fellow'. White, born in Drogheda, Ireland, had once worked in his father's business as a slater and tiler, but a fondness for the sea had

The murder of Sir John Dineley Goodere. (Contemporary engraving/British Library)

led him to be taken on as a cabin boy, and he had served on many ships. It was said of him he never stayed in a port for a week without providing himself with a new wife. After squandering her money he would leave her with only a foul disease as a memento. White was called from his hammock at 1 a.m. to the captain's cabin and given a dram of rum, and then several more, and was told he had to murder a madman. Money was provided – a thirty-six-shilling piece of gold – and more promised. The plan was to put to sea after the murder, when the body could be sewn into a hammock and thrown over the side. Samuel provided a rope, White made a noose in it and a handkerchief was supplied to put over Sir John's mouth. Samuel then lit the men with a candle to the cabin door where Buchanan was still standing sentry, took the cutlass from him, and told him to go and walk on deck. Samuel stood sentry while White and Mahony entered the room. Sir John was lying on the bed. At first Mahony casually asked him how his head was, but after a moment or two of conversation said that it did not signify talking about it any longer. Sir John knew his last moments had come. In a final effort to stave off death he offered his implacable murderers money, crying out 'Twenty guineas! Take it! Must I die? Must I die?' On the other side of the partition, Jones the cooper was awoken by his wife. 'Don't you hear the noise that is being made by the gentleman? I believe they are killing him.' There was a sound of kicking and struggling, and Jones peered through a crack in the partition, but the room was dark. Fearful that they would be killed if they stirred from their room, they remained silent.

According to White, it was Mahony who started to strangle Sir John with his bare hands, but Mahony's story was that it was the stronger White who did so, while he held the man down. White then put the rope around their victim's neck while Mahony hauled on it and made it tight 'for fear he should not be dead enough'. The deed done, White took a knife from his pocket and cut the rope off. It was later thrown overboard.

The sounds also awoke Dudgeon, the surgeon's mate. He too suspected murder, but knowing that there was an armed man outside the door, he dared not interfere. Buchanan, who had attributed the noises to a fit of madness, brought a candle to the captain, but Samuel waved the cutlass at him and told him to go back. Later, when all was quiet, Samuel called for a candle and handed it in to Mahony. Inside the cabin White and Mahony were rifling the pockets of their victim, finding a watch and £30 in cash. The light enabled Jones to see the two men robbing what he was sure was a corpse. 'Have ye done?' asked Samuel; then he came into the room. Jones did not see who this third man was, but he saw a hand touching the throat of the victim – not the hand of a common sailor, but whiter. He heard the words, ''Tis done, and well done.'

Samuel left the cabin, gave Buchanan the cutlass and told him to stand guard and to call him if his brother made a noise. He then locked the door and took away the key. Back in his own cabin Samuel prepared for bed. Calling Mahony and White to him, he gave them another five guineas and said they could keep the money they had taken from the corpse, although he took his brother's watch and gave them his own in its place. He told the men they would have to go away for three weeks, and he would send them their tickets. The *Ruby*'s yawl (the ship's boat) was due to go to the city between 4 and 5 a.m. and he expected them to be on it.

Jones and his wife, both shaking with terror, finally dared to emerge from their cabin and went to see Dudgeon. He suggested that they check to see whether Sir John was dead, and so they drew aside the scuttle (the hatch that looked into the purser's cabin from the steward's room), called out to the man inside and tried to

Cover of a pamphlet about the murder.
(Contemporary publication/British Library)

move him with a stick, but there was no sign of life. Certain now that murder had been committed, they decided to speak to a senior officer, Lieutenant William Parry, but Parry, who had a good opinion of his captain, refused to believe their story. 'It can't be so,' he said. 'I don't believe the captain would do any such thing.' Just then Mr Marsh the midshipman arrived and said that there were orders from the captain that Mahony and White should be carried to shore. Jones insisted that something should be done. He said that if Parry would do nothing, he himself would write to the Admiralty and the mayor of Bristol. Unshaken, Parry proceeded to order the carrying-out of the captain's instructions, and White and Mahony were duly transported ashore to the Gibb, where they arrived at 6 a.m.

THE GENUINE

MEMOIRS

OF THE

LIFE

OF

Sir JOHN DINELY GOODERE, Bart.

WHO WAS

Murder'd by the Contrivance of his own Brother,

On Board the

RUBY Man of War,

IN

King-Road near Bristol, Jan. 19, 17⁴0.

Together with the

LIFE, HISTORY, TRYAL,

AND

Laſt Dying WORDS,

Of His Brother

Capt. SAMUEL GOODERE,

WHO WAS

Executed at BRISTOL, on Wednesday the 15th Day of April, 1741, for the horrid Murder of the ſaid Sir JOHN DINELY GOODERE, Bart.

DEDICATED to the Right Worſhipful HENRY COMBE, Eſq; Mayor of Briſtol.

By S. FOOTE, of Worceſter-College, Oxford, Eſq; and Nephew to the late Sir John Dinely Goodere, Bart.

LONDON:

Printed and Sold by T. Cooper, in Pater-noſter-Row. 1741.

⌐ Price Six Pence. ⌐

That morning Jarrit Smith went to see the mayor of the city, Henry Combe, and asked him to dispatch an officer to search the *Ruby* before it left the liberty of the city. By now Jones had reported his suspicions to Theodore Court, the ship's master, and the ship was in an uproar. Parry, Court and Jones discussed what to do. Parry, still unable to believe what he heard, advised caution, as he did not want to arrest the captain without being sure that Sir John was dead. 'I shall be broke, and you too,' he said. At 8 a.m. Parry breakfasted with Samuel in his cabin. Soon afterwards a shore boat arrived with armed men led by Thomas Chamberlayne. The door of the purser's cabin was broken open, and Chamberlayne saw Sir John lying dead, with rope marks on his neck and blood coming from his mouth and nose. With murder no longer in doubt, men were at once sent ashore to find Mahony and White.

A plan was then devised to secure Samuel, who was still in his cabin. Jones requested permission to see Samuel with a complaint, saying that his sea chest had been broken open and items stolen. Samuel agreed to see him, and as the captain paced the room with his hands held behind him, Jones rushed up and seized him. Several other men then ran in and Samuel was secured. 'Sir,' said Jones, 'you are my prisoner.' Parry, who later became an admiral, was never able to the end of his life to speak about the events of that day without weeping.

White and Mahony were found before long, White at the Bell Inn and Mahony in a house opposite the Ship Inn on St Michael's Hill. Both were so drunk it was impossible to question them until the following day. On the morning of Tuesday 20 January 1741 two coroners and a jury arrived on board the *Ruby*, where they held the inquest and brought in a verdict of murder against White, Mahony and Samuel Goodere. Later that day an armed guard conducted the captain to Bristol.

When Samuel Goodere was brought for questioning to the Council House he arrived with a smile and a swagger. He bowed to the mayor, then to the aldermen and magistrates, many of whom he knew, declaring that he was as innocent of the matter as they were. He knew nothing of the taking of Sir John and suggested that his brother had committed suicide while insane. It was a great hardship, he said, for an innocent man, and he hoped one day to be able to punish those who did him such an injustice. He was unable, however, to refute the evidence with which he was confronted, and was committed to Bristol's Newgate Gaol, also known as the City Gaol for Debtors and Malefactors. Situated at the eastern end of Wine Street, it had a reputation for appallingly insanitary conditions. On arrival Samuel informed the keeper that he would not be staying there long, as he would get bail, but he was advised that since the inquest had found him and his accomplices guilty of murder, this was not possible. At this news some of his cheerful demeanour vanished. Had he been bailed, Samuel would undoubtedly have absconded. Failing this, he engaged in a series of increasingly desperate attempts to evade justice. On his being searched not long afterwards, some knives and other instruments were discovered in his coat pocket which he could have used to kill himself, or, more probably, effect an escape. From that moment he was watched very carefully. Samuel next wrote to his friends and any person of influence he knew, including two members of the House of Commons, one of whom was a distant relation, appealing to them to help him. All of them declined.

Having failed to avoid going to trial, Samuel next tried to get the trial held not in the city of Bristol but at an Admiralty session, where presumably he thought he might get a more favourable result. After a lengthy correspondence between the Solicitor to the Admiralty and Sir Michael Foster, the Recorder of Bristol, it was established that the location of the ship at the time of the murder was within the county of Bristol, and that therefore the trial should take place there. The proceedings were due to commence on 18 March 1741, but Samuel next claimed, through his physician, Dr Middleton, that he was too ill to undergo the fatigue of a trial. Mr Vernon, King's Counsel, smelled a device and asked if the prisoner was well enough to come to court to enter a plea. Middleton said he was, and on the following day Samuel was brought into court and pleaded not guilty. This enabled Mr Vernon to have a good look at him, and he observed dryly that Samuel looked able enough to take his trial. An adjournment of one week was

Sir Michael Foster.
(Contemporary
engraving/British
Library)

allowed, and the trial opened on 26 March before Sir Michael Foster. Samuel and
Mahony were being tried together, with White to take his trial separately on the
following day. Jarrit Smith was present, both as a witness and as the solicitor for
the prosecution.

Samuel tried to open the proceedings with a statement to the court, but it was
quickly pointed out that this was both irregular and improper. Mr Vernon gave
an able recapitulation of the facts in his opening address, and then Samuel's
counsel, Mr Shepherd, put it to the court that since in the indictment Sir John had
been referred to only by his name, and not by his title of baronet, he was
improperly described, and the prisoners could not therefore be found guilty on
the indictment. Oddly enough, he failed to mention that Samuel, who was now
3rd Baronet, had not been given his title on the indictment either. Sir Michael
gave this idea very short shrift, saying it was quite sufficient for Sir John to be
described by his Christian name and surname. 'I would not deny the prisoners
any advantage they are by law entitled to,' he said, 'but I cannot admit of
evidence which can serve only to amuse.'

Samuel was entitled to question the witnesses, and when Theodore Court, the ship's master, gave evidence he asked him where the ship lay and how the winds blew, in a vain effort to promote the old argument that at the time of the murder the ship had not been within the jurisdiction of the city. 'I should be very sorry', said Mr Vernon, 'to find the jurisdiction of a city . . . shaken by a side–wind, and hope any attempt of this nature will not be suffered.'

Samuel next attempted to show that Sir John had been insane and that the reason for his detention was to treat his affliction. A Mrs Gethins testified that two or three weeks before the murder Samuel had asked if he could rent a garret from her in which to keep his brother, who was a madman. Mr Vernon asked her whether her garret was a proper place of accommodation for a gentleman and an English baronet. 'Pray do you keep a mad-house, Madam?' he asked, to which she could only answer 'No.'

Some of Sir John's servants gave evidence that their master had carried out many acts of lunacy, throwing things at them and accusing them of coming to shoot him. This was countered by Jarrit Smith, who said he had known Sir John for fourteen or fifteen years and always believed him to be a man of sound understanding.

Samuel, his confidence still undented, announced, 'I shall not give your Lordship and the jury much trouble. I am entirely innocent; they have not proved that I was present at the death of Sir John Dineley.' 'Don't deceive yourself,' said Sir Michael. 'Though they have not proved that you was [sic] in the cabin, when Sir John was murdered, yet they have given evidence of that which (if the Jury give credit to) will amount to presence in the eye of the law.'

After some character witnesses spoke in Samuel's favour there was a last-ditch attempt to prove that the ship was not within the city and county of Bristol, which ploy Sir Michael stamped upon very firmly.

Mahony then made a very poor showing, claiming he was a penniless pressed servant, and had made the confession when drunk and frightened. Sir Michael pointed out to him that he had been drunk when arrested but had been allowed to sober up before being questioned. Mahony had no witnesses to call.

When Mr Vernon addressed the court he made the important point that although Samuel Goodere said he wasn't present at the time of Sir John's death, the law stated that if several persons are engaged in a design to murder another and one stands watch, he is considered to be present at the act, and as much a principal in it as the others. In this, Sir Michael emphatically concurred in his summing-up. The jury were absent for only fifteen minutes before they found both prisoners guilty.

After the trial Samuel Goodere returned to Newgate. He wore a scarlet cloak, and as he walked through the streets he paused to bow to any members of the gentry or persons of his acquaintance. It was feared that he had made arrangements for a last-minute rescue, so officers were posted to prevent this. In the event nothing happened. Condemned convicts were usually thrown into an underground dungeon known as the Pit, although it is possible that Samuel was

Bristol Harbour, 1782. (Contemporary print/British Library)

accorded a rather better apartment owing to his rank. A new, iron-plated door was installed, watched by guards in case of an attack on the prison.

White was tried on the following day. He pleaded not guilty, claiming to recall nothing of the murder, as he had been drunk. This didn't impress the court, and he too was found guilty. On 28 March all three men were sentenced to hang. Samuel's wife at once petitioned for the sentence of death to be mitigated to imprisonment or transportation, but without success.

Two clergymen, Mr Weston (curate of St Peter's) and Mr Penrose, came to preach to Samuel, but at first he continued to declare he was innocent of murder. On 8 April a coffin was carried into his room, inscribed 'Samuel Goodere, aged 53 years who departed this life April 15 1741'. This must have had a sobering effect. As a sense of the inevitable came upon him, Samuel sought the comfort of religion. His manner became more serious; he read pious books and asked for religious instruction. Ultimately he admitted his guilt, owned that his sentence was just, and expressed great sorrow and repentance for what he had done.

Mahony, who seemed to have been judged the most guilty of the three, was due to be hanged in irons after the execution. He languished in jail, showing a surly and brutish temper, but perhaps the process of being measured for his irons sobered him a little. He gradually became more thoughtful and eventually made a full confession. White's burly belligerence had vanished with the sentence, and he spent his time weeping and praying.

At 11 a.m. on the morning of 15 April the prisoners, with halters around their necks, were taken to be executed. Samuel Goodere was conveyed in a mourning chariot through one of the greatest crowds Bristol had ever seen, with a similarly large assembly at the place of execution on St Michael's Hill. Mahony and White were taken in a cart, together with 22-year-old Jane Williams, who had been convicted of murdering her child after being abandoned by the man who had seduced her. Samuel confessed to his crime and expressed his penitence. After psalms and prayers he thanked the minister and took his leave of the acquaintances around him. He embraced Mahony and White and said he was sorry to have been the means of bringing them to their untimely end. The prisoners were tied. At Samuel's signal, the dropping of a handkerchief, the cart on which they stood drew away, and as they struggled their last the onlookers prayed. There was some concern that at this last moment there might be an attempt to revive Samuel, so his body was allowed to hang for an hour and a quarter before being cut down and taken in a hearse to the infirmary at Newgate where, in the presence of as many spectators as could be crammed in, a surgeon stuck a scalpel in its chest. There it lay all night, and on the following day the remains of Samuel Goodere were taken to be buried in the family vault in Herefordshire. Mahony's body was gibbeted on Dunball Island near the scene of the murder, but White was buried in St James's Churchyard.

After the executions Samuel's widow wrote to her cousin for mourning clothes to be made 'in the very pink of ye mode', yet she also expressed her grief: '. . . itt have all mostt ben my Deth,' she wrote, 'for I am fritt outt of my wits.' The newspaper accounts of the event were, she claimed, 'very ill ritt', adding, 'I have a greatt deall to say butt my Hartt is to full.' Elizabeth was said to have died a little over a year after the execution.

The baronetcy passed to Samuel's eldest son, Edward, who died insane aged 32 in 1761, and then to his second son, John, who frittered away the estate and died unmarried in 1809. With his demise the baronetcy became extinct.

3

A SHOT IN THE DARK

Catgrove Wood, Hill, near Berkeley, 1816

The popular image of the poacher is that of the poor but resourceful countryman, bagging game for the pot to feed his family. While there is some truth in this, it was a very different species of poacher that troubled the parish of Hill in the early nineteenth century. Poaching was an industry, in which pheasants were sold on to private dealers and eventually appeared on the tables of city gentlemen, who did not enquire too closely as to the origins of their dinner. The profits were further spiced by the thrill of night-time excursions, when the men would blacken their faces and chalk secret marks on their hats to aid mutual identification. The Hill poachers' ringleader was 27-year-old John Allen of Lower Moreton (now spelt Morton), who by day was both a farmer and a tax collector. Allen was an educated man, a close friend of his near neighbour, William Adams Brodribb, the local attorney, and the owner of a weighty compendium of general

Lower Morton. (Author's collection)

knowledge – *The Young Man's Best Companion*, which included chapters on arithmetic, algebra, bookkeeping, geometry, geography and astronomy. Outwardly respectable, Allen had a rebellious, reckless streak which took him into the woods at night with lawless companions and a gun.

So outraged were the landowners at the poachers' depredations that they took the unusual and dangerous step of protecting their woodlands with spring-guns, devices with a wire attached to the trigger. It was only a matter of time before tragedy struck. On 25 November 1815 Thomas Till, a 28-year-old labourer of Crossways, was looking for game in Prestwood, land belonging to Lord Ducie, when he tripped a spring-gun. He received five wounds in his left side and was killed instantly. At the inquest, which took place on the following day at the Royal Oak Inn, Cromhall, it was pointed out that warning notices had been posted on boards outside the wood. The inquest jury considered the case very carefully for most of the day before returning a verdict of accidental death. This did nothing to deter the neighbourhood poachers; rather it firmed their resolve to take revenge for the death of Thomas Till, who had left a grieving widow with two small children to care for.

That December John Allen boasted to a neighbour, John Jones, that he would soon be 'paying a visit' to Miss Florence Langley, mistress of nearby Hill Court and its estate, as he knew where her game was. Jones told him to 'leave it off', as he was sure to be taken. Allen, full of bravado, replied that he would sooner shoot a man than be taken; in fact, he went on, he would sooner die than be taken. Jones was not impressed.

On Thursday 11 January 1816 Allen asked his servant, William Greenaway, to recruit some men for a poaching expedition to Miss Langley's manor and Catgrove Wood, the property of Colonel Berkeley. No date was then mentioned. One of the men Greenaway recruited was John Penny, a hot-headed 24-year-old labourer of Littleton-on-Severn, who already had a conviction for poaching.

The proposed expedition was not a subject for private conversation; rather it was discussed openly in the street. On the evening of Thursday 18 January Greenaway was talking to Henry Reeves, a labourer of Moreton as he came out of his father's yard, when Allen, who was in his orchard, called out, 'Henry, will you go? Your brother John and Anthony Barton are going.' He then revealed that the party was to meet at his house at 10 p.m. Just then John Burley, Greenaway's 19-year-old stepson, came whistling along the road. Allen had already stipulated that the lad was not to be one of the party, so the men quickly returned to their homes, but their behaviour at once aroused Burley's suspicions.

Later that evening Allen ordered Greenaway to saddle his horse. While this was being done Allen asked him to go with the party, and it was arranged that Greenaway would come to Allen's house at 9 p.m. Allen then rode away. Greenaway arrived shortly before nine, but the only people present were Miss Nelmes, the elderly lady who owned the house, and Allen's wife and children. After waiting a while Greenaway went to a nearby house occupied by John Reeves, the 28-year-old brother of Henry, and Anthony Barton, a farmer and pig

Hill Court, home of Miss Florence Langley. (Author's collection)

butcher. He warned the men that they should not go directly to Allen's house, because Burley and a friend of his, James Jenkins (a 21-year-old Moreton labourer), who was also to be excluded, might see them and suspect something. He returned to Allen's, and gradually the new arrivals started to trickle in. Brothers Thomas and William Collins, farmers of Littleton, and John Penny and his older brother, William, all brought guns. Daniel Long, a 23-year-old farmer of Hill, arrived carrying a stick. The next arrivals were nothing to do with the expedition, and initially may not have known anything about it. These were attorney William Brodribb, who had probably come to see Allen on a business matter, and two neighbours, Mr Hasell and Dr Kean.

It was after ten before Allen arrived. 'How d'ye do, gentlemen?' he said, and placed powder and shot on the table, saying it amounted to sixty charges in all. Asked for flints, he produced some from his pocket, and everyone who had a gun took one. Even Brodribb joined in, putting a flint into one of the guns. By now it must have been quite apparent to Brodribb what was to happen that night, but he seemed not to be uncomfortable about it.

Greenaway, still anxious about Burley and Jenkins, went outside and, finding Anthony Barton and John Reeves in the orchard, invited them to come in. Barton had already blacked his face, which suggested to the others that this would be a good idea, so they did likewise. By now the little group had become quite a throng, swelled by the arrival of James Roach, a 24-year-old farmer's son of Thornbury, Thomas Morgan, a 24-year-old mason of Littleton, Robert Groves, just 19, who managed his widowed mother's farm, and Thomas and John Hayward, sons of a Moreton farmer.

It was now proposed (no one could later remember by whom) that the men should all swear an oath that they would not 'peach' on each other, and the obvious man to administer that oath was the man of law, Brodribb. Brodribb later claimed that he had at first objected strongly to the idea, although no one else recalled him being other than quite willing to comply. He went into the kitchen and fetched a book. The men were duly sworn and kissed the book, two or three being sworn at once, each holding on to a corner. 'You shall not peach on each other, so help you God' were the words Brodribb was alleged to have said, although he later denied he had said 'so help you God'. All the men were under the impression that they had sworn a solemn oath on the Holy Bible. They had actually (and this was a deliberate subterfuge on Brodribb's part) sworn it on *The Young Man's Best Companion*.

Their hats were then chalked with letters and a white spot on the front, except for Allen's, which, presumably in acknow-ledgement of his leadership, was chalked with a king's crown. Allen, who had decided not to carry a gun, gave his to one of the Collins brothers, while a spare gun of John Penny's was given to Greenaway. Barton, Reeves and both Haywards also had guns. It was then found that Burley and Jenkins had not failed to notice what was afoot and had been hanging about the area, hoping to join in the excitement. There was some debate about letting them come. In the end it was agreed they could, so they were brought in and their faces blacked. Dr Kean oblig-ingly chalked their hats for them, and

Title page of The Young Man's [Best] Companion. *(Contemporary publication/British Library)*

Grounds of Hill Court. (Author's collection)

Brodribb administered the oath. One of the gentlemen then said he would like to see the men in a line, so they were accordingly formed into a line.

There were now sixteen men in the party. They left Allen's house by the back door and headed towards Hill. It was 10.30 p.m., frosty underfoot, and a bright, moonlit night, easily light enough to see and be seen. At Hill, the pheasants roosting in the bare branches of the trees were easy targets, and a few were shot and killed. The men were by now in exuberant mood and were making no effort to conceal their activities. When one of their number warned that keepers had been seen in the area, Barton said loudly, 'If any of our party runs I will blow his leg or arm off!' They marched on to Catgrove.

The men had already been seen. George Hancock, a tailor of Hill, and Henry Hobby, a labourer, were in the lane between Hill Court and Allen's house when they heard the crunch of tramping feet on the icy road and stopped to listen. The next sounds were of men climbing over a hedge, followed by shots. They then saw the men at the top of the lane, firing more shots which, alarmingly, seemed to go over their heads. While Hancock was unable to recognise anyone, he knew Allen, and just the previous Christmas had heard him boasting that he would have some of Miss Langley's game, and that he had a knife to cut the ears of her keeper. He was in little doubt as to who was leading the gang. Hancock knew that Colonel Berkeley's keepers were to be found at the Round House in Round House Wood, which lay between Moreton and Catgrove, and at once ran there to alert them, only to find that they had already departed.

Catgrove Wood was, and indeed still is, accessible from the south by a gate leading to a path known as the main ride, which went due north through the wood. Two other narrower roads led off the main ride to the west, one immediately inside the gate and the second a little further on. The party of poachers boldly entered the wood through the gate and crept up the main ride. Sensing game, they turned left into the second path, and a number of shots had been fired when they suddenly become aware that they were not alone.

Catgrove Wood, the main ride looking north into the wood from the gate. (Author's collection)

Lord Ducie, Miss Langley and Colonel Berkeley had already heard whispers that a party of poachers was to go out that night and had assembled a group of nineteen gamekeepers at the Round House. At the insistence of Colonel Berkeley none of the men carried guns but were armed only with stout sticks, mostly common walking sticks. To recognise each other in the dark, they had handkerchiefs or tapes tied around their arms. The keepers had marched as a group up to the wicket gate at the corner of Round House Wood before separating into two parties, Lord Ducie's ten and the Colonel's nine. A newspaper account later suggested that there was also a group of eleven men supplied by Miss Langley, but it seemed that they went further off and took no part in the ensuing affray.

Thomas Clarke, the Colonel's park keeper, led the Colonel's men, who included William Ingram, the assistant gamekeeper. They entered Catgrove Wood by the main gate and soon heard guns firing from within the wood, followed by the sound of fluttering wings. Anticipating a confrontation, they took off their great-coats and flung them to the ground, so as to have greater freedom of movement. Unsure of exactly where the poachers were, they split into two groups, some of the men turning into the first lane while others took the main ride. It was this second group, led by Clarke, with Ingram at his side, who peered down the second lane on the left and saw the party of poachers only some 15 yards away. The poachers, realising they had been spotted, huddled together and whispered 'Whish, whish, whish!' to show that they had seen the gamekeepers. In that moment of quiet tension there could have been many possible outcomes, but matters were put beyond doubt by one of the poachers firing a gun. Clarke, careless of possible injury, stepped forward into the middle of the ride, flourished his stick and cried, 'Huzza, my boys, fight like men!' Ingram moved up to take his place, and the rest of the Colonel's gamekeepers, hearing Clarke's shout, ran up to join him. The poachers levelled their guns and, with Greenaway at the front, flanked on one side by John Allen and on the other by John Penny, advanced until the two groups of men were only some 8 yards apart.

At Clarke's rallying cry Lord Ducie's men, who were not far away, rushed up to join the other keepers, but before they could arrive a second shot rang out. William Ingram suddenly drew himself up and fell to the ground, where he gave two little gasps and died. Seconds later the poachers fired again. This time Clarke was wounded in the thigh, and another man, Charles Davis, was hit in the head and eyes. The poachers now moved steadily forward, the keepers making a gradual retreat until both groups were in the main ride. Here the keepers held their ground, and the poachers formed a line across the width of the ride. From this position the poachers could easily have made their escape by turning around and heading north but, as if by some unspoken agreement, they chose to make their exit the way they had come, and that meant driving a path through the gamekeepers. There was a pause of about a minute as the two opposing groups faced each other. Then five or six shots rang out, wounding five more game-keepers in the legs. The entire body of poachers now made a run forward and

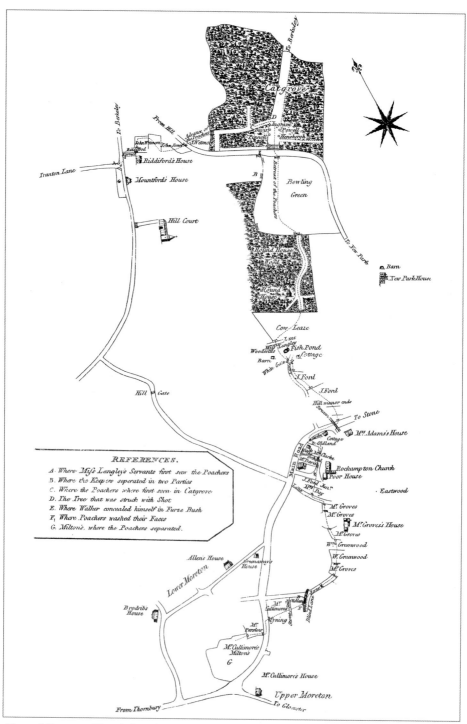

Map of Catgrove Wood showing where the murder took place, the route taken by the poachers and the houses of Allen, Greenaway and Brodribb. (Contemporary drawing/ British Library)

there was confusion as poachers and gamekeepers intermingled and blows were exchanged with sticks. The poachers kept together but some of the keepers scattered, while others stood their ground and traded blows with the poachers. Thomas Clarke, unable to run, was struck on the shoulder. Gamekeeper James Hensbergh had been hit in the leg and hip, but as the poachers ran past him he was sure that despite their blacked faces he recognised a man he had known for some four years – John Allen.

The poachers ran out through the main gate and on in the direction of Round House Wood. In great high spirits, they marched on boldly at a good pace, down the Bowling-Green and on to the steep ground of the Cow Leaze. 'Now', said John Penny, 'Tom Till's debts are paid', and another man cried out 'Glory!' They stopped briefly at a stream to wash their faces and clean their hats. Before the men went their separate ways Allen urged that they again take an oath not to tell – even their dearest friend on earth – or they would all be hanged if found out. With that sobering thought the men returned to their homes. Greenaway, at Allen's instructions, hid some of the guns under the straw in Allen's cow-house and then went home to bed, where, soon afterwards, he heard the clock strike one. Allen went on to Brodribb's, where he was confident that the attorney and his two friends might provide him with an alibi.

The following morning Allen was calmly weighing flour in the back kitchen when a neighbour, John Meachin, arrived with the news of what had happened the previous night, reporting that one man had been killed and eight wounded. 'They should bide at home, like me,' was Allen's comment. After Meachin left Greenaway confided that he was sorry for what had happened, but Allen's reply was 'The sons of bitches should bide at home.'

In the morning light George Hancock and Henry Hobby followed the footprints which were still clearly visible in the frost and found that they led from Catgrove Wood all the way to the Moreton road, where they could no longer be seen, but Hobby went on to Allen's house and found the tracks of many men outside.

On the morning of Saturday 20 January 1816 twenty men, led by an irate and determined Colonel Berkeley, rode up to John Allen's house and quickly surrounded it. Allen, who had seen the men approach, quickly bolted the front door, then ran to the back exit to make his escape. By the time he got there, however, he found that Thomas Clarke, who was not too badly injured to be one of the party, was waiting for him. Allen bolted that door, too, and retreated inside. Clarke returned to the front of the house, where the Colonel, who was armed with a pistol, was shouting out that he would take Allen dead or alive. Allen appeared at a window. 'What do you want me for?' he asked.

'For murder,' was the reply. Allen said nothing but disappeared inside the house again. The Colonel demanded that Allen surrender himself and threatened to break the door down. Allen refused to emerge, so the gamekeepers eventually started to force the door. It was by now obvious to Allen that there was no escape. Once again he came to the window and said he would surrender himself on condition that no one laid hands upon him, but Colonel Berkeley was in no mood to meet any conditions. Finally the door gave way, and Allen, who must have been terrified that he would be shot on sight if he attempted to show any resistance, appeared with his hands in his pockets. The Colonel at once seized him by the collar and gave him into the charge of two of his men to be taken to Hill Court to be examined by Mr Cheston, the magistrate. Just as Allen was being led away the Colonel heard the sound of footsteps behind him and a voice crying, 'They shall not take him! They shall not take him!' He turned round and saw Greenaway running up, looking as if he might be about to strike him. The Colonel did not wait to see if Greenaway would hit him, but knocked him flat on the ground with a single punch. Greenaway was hauled to his feet and taken to the magistrates at Hill Court on a charge of attempting to rescue Allen.

When examined by Mr Cheston both men denied all knowledge of the murder. Allen claimed that he and his three friends, Mr Hasell, Dr Kean and Mr Brodribb, had all been at his house until 9 p.m., after which they had all gone on to Brodribb's and stayed there till 1.30 a.m., smoking and drinking. Those three were, he claimed, his only companions that evening. Cheston was sure that Allen and Greenaway knew more than they were saying; they were taken to Berkeley Castle and placed in the dungeons.

Berkeley Castle. (Author's collection)

On the same day the inquest into the death of William Ingram opened at New Park Farm, Berkeley. Mr Jenner, the surgeon, had examined the body and confirmed that Ingram had died of gunshot wounds – the kind of common game-shot used to kill hares. At the time of his death Ingram was 26 and had been in service with Colonel Berkeley for five years. He had married Ann Kitterell in 1813, and a son, William, was born the following year. Daniel Long, one of the poachers, had been a witness at his wedding. The inquest heard that a portion of the charge had entered Ingram's heart, and he had died almost instantly. The jury returned a verdict of wilful murder but, with enquiries proceeding, declined to name a culprit. Ingram was buried at Stone on 24 January.

The authorities, sure that John Allen was the ringleader, were unwilling to offer him a pardon in return for information, but Greenaway was another matter. For several days, despite being repeatedly asked to confess, he continued to stand by his oath. But as the other poachers were gradually rounded up and joined him in Berkeley Castle, and James Prewett, the Thornbury coachman, who had not been involved, was arrested on suspicion, Greenaway began to waver.

Colonel Berkeley and his men were still on the hunt for the remainder of the gang. He had engaged the services of a Bow Street policeman, John Vickery, who arrived at the castle on Sunday 21 January and was dispatched to find the malefactors. He was unable to find the Haywards, but at Thornbury he found James Roach cowering half-dressed in a cellar, and dragged him out.

On the same day William Brodribb was asked to go to the castle and give his account of what had happened that night. Brodribb was only 26 at the time, and despite his education and family commitments – he was married with three children – seems to have shared some of his friend Allen's rebellious spirit. Boldly, he told the magistrate that Lord Ducie and Colonel Berkeley had brought it all on themselves by setting the traps, and he did not think that any of the men would have thought of firing at the gamekeepers if one of their own men had not previously been killed. Mr Cheston observed that he thought Mr Brodribb knew more about the murder than he was saying, at which the young attorney backtracked rapidly, apologised for his statements and admitted that the actions of the poachers were not justified. To his relief he was allowed to go home.

William Penny and Thomas Collins decided on a bluff. On the Wednesday after the shooting (24 January) they went voluntarily to the castle to be questioned, hoping that their cooperation would be seen as a sign of innocence. It was not, and they were both detained. For two days they were asked to confess but insisted they knew nothing about the incident. By then the authorities were sure they had their men, and they were both hand-bolted and fettered together.

John Burley had initially escaped to Bristol on Allen's horse but, on hearing he was wanted for questioning, made his way to the castle, where he denied all knowledge of the events of the fatal night. He was incarcerated with the others. On the night of Friday 26 January Daniel Long, John Reeves and Thomas Morgan were all apprehended.

William Greenaway had spent several solitary days in the dungeons pondering his fate, and when he learned that there was eyewitness evidence from George Hancock and others to identify the gang, he realised there was only one way to save his life and that of his stepson. Urged by Mr Cheston to make a full declaration in return for a free pardon, he agreed, on condition that John Burley was also included. 'It would be hard,' he observed, 'to hang my own flesh and blood.' Young Burley, even after he knew of the pardon, stuck to his oath and said nothing, even when Vickery told him he was sure to hang if he remained silent.

Greenaway's statement revealed Brodribb's part in the affair, and a warrant was issued for his arrest on a charge of administering an unlawful oath. On Sunday 28 January the attorney was brought back to the castle, where Greenaway's statement was read out to him. He admitted he had administered the oath but said he had been very careful that the book he used was not a Testament. This did not impress Mr Cheston, and Brodribb was committed to prison.

Still missing was John Penny, one of the men who had been at the front of the group of poachers and who, Greenaway said, had fired the shot that killed Ingram. It was known that Penny's wife was resident wet-nurse with a Bristol family called Bryan, and on 28 January Vickery went to question her, accompanied by a Bristol officer called Smith. It was 7 p.m. when Vickery knocked boldly on the door. On being admitted he advised Mr Bryan of the reason for his visit. Mrs Penny was duly brought to him and did not conceal the fact that her husband was in the house. Penny was in the downstairs kitchen; Vickery, listening from the hallway, could hear his quarry in conversation with the maidservants. Reckoning that if he could hear Penny then Penny could hear him, Vickery announced loudly that he had come to arrest John Penny on suspicion of murdering William Ingram. Vickery and Smith were then conducted down to the kitchen by the Bryans, Mrs Penny anxiously following. They found Penny standing with his back to the fire in 'an attitude of defence'.

Vickery calmly produced an arrest warrant and invited Penny to accompany him. As expected, he was met by a torrent of bad language, and it was very obvious that Penny was prepared to use violence to avoid being taken. Unperturbed, Vickery informed Penny that he would read the warrant to him, and proceeded to do so. This was followed by an attempt to apprehend the suspect, which Penny resisted by kicking out at the policeman, and Vickery was obliged to strike Penny twice. Mrs Penny suddenly threw herself at her desperate husband, clung to him and begged him to go quietly, while the Bryans made a similar plea, but without effect. Vickery drew a pistol and said that if Penny resisted arrest or tried to strike him he would shoot. This provoked another bout of bad language from Penny, the general drift of which was that Vickery might shoot if he pleased. In the meantime, Smith had gone to get assistance, and when this arrived, Penny was at once overcome by sheer numbers, and his hands were tied. The prisoner struggled and swore, accusing first his wife and then the Bryans of having sent for the police, both of which suggestions Vickery firmly refuted. Dragged bodily into the street, Penny did everything he could to resist, struggling, kicking out at the policemen, trying to trip them up and even attempting to throw himself to the ground as a dead weight. As crowds gathered he cried out that he was being taken for poaching only, and Vickery, to avert a possible rescue attempt, told the mob that he was arresting the murderer of Colonel Berkeley's keeper. Penny was taken to a secure lock-up, every step of the way being hauled by main force.

The following morning Penny was in calmer mood and apologised for his violent behaviour. When brought before Mr Cheston he gave a rambling, contradictory statement, which was carefully recorded as he spoke. Denying that he was the murderer, he added, 'I do not say whether I am innocent or not.' He said that Greenaway was mistaken as to who was there that night and claimed that he could bring witnesses to give him an alibi. As was later pointed out, if he had not been involved he could hardly have known whether Greenaway was mistaken or not.

About a fortnight after the murder Robert Groves was found in Monmouthshire and brought back, protesting his innocence. He was hand-bolted and put into the dungeons with the rest. Four of the party were never found – William Collins, Anthony Barton, and John and Thomas Hayward. It was reputed that the Haywards had sailed for America.

When the trial opened at the Gloucester Assizes before Mr Justice Holroyd on Tuesday 9 April there was the unique sight of eleven men in the dock on a capital charge. All the men were charged with assault. John Penny was specifically charged with shooting Ingram, the others with aiding and abetting him. In an alternative charge John Allen was accused of the shooting. They all pleaded not guilty. Mr Dauncey for the prosecution said he had never seen a trial of life and death in which there were so many prisoners. He established from the first that where several persons jointly engage in an illegal act, and death ensues from it, then 'they are all answerable'.

Several of the keepers gave their account of the events of the fatal night. George Hancock and Henry Hobby told how they had followed the tracks of the poachers the morning after the shooting, and Hancock and John Jones repeated Allen's boasts that he would have some of Miss Langley's game.

The witnesses for the defence were not especially helpful. Mark Biddle, who had been arrested on suspicion on 20 January and released after three days in the castle cells, claimed that he had been offered 200 guineas and a pardon to name the company of poachers, and that he had heard Greenaway being offered a similar reward. Biddle had previously been in jail for poaching, and when arrested had a rabbit net in his pocket. Seventeen witnesses were brought to attest to the excellent character of the defendants, but during questioning it was revealed that Allen was very fond of shooting and game, and that John Penny had once been in jail for poaching.

Summing up, Mr Justice Holroyd advised the jury that the identity of the man who fired the fatal shot was immaterial, 'the act of any one being the act of all . . . All the men in this case, who united to force a way through the keepers, with

THE
TRIAL AT LARGE
OF

John Penny,	Daniel Long,	James Roach,
William Penny,	John Reeves,	Robert Groves,
Thomas Collins,	James Jenkins,	AND
John Allen,	Thomas Morgan,	John Burley,

FOR THE

𝕎ilful 𝕄urder of 𝕎. 𝕀ngram,

(GAMEKEEPER TO COLONEL BERKELEY,)

At Catgrove, in the Parish of Hill, Gloucestershire:

—»⟶⊙⟵«—

LIKEWISE, THE

Trial of W. A. Brodribb, Gentleman,

For administering an Unlawful Oath

TO THE ABOVE PERSONS.

AT

GLOUCESTER LENT ASSIZES, 1816,

Before the Hon. Mr. Justice Holroyd.

TO WHICH IS PREFIXED,

AN INTRODUCTORY NARRATIVE

Of the Circumstances which led to the Apprehension of the Offenders,

And a Plan of the Ground

On which the Murder was committed.

GLOUCESTER:

PRINTED AND SOLD BY D. WALKER AND SONS,

JOURNAL-OFFICE, WESTGATE-STREET;

SOLD ALSO BY SHERWOOD, NEELY, & JONES, PATERNOSTER-ROW, LONDON;
AND MAY BE HAD OF ALL OTHER BOOKSELLERS.

Price 3s.

Title page of the published account of the poachers' trial. (Contemporary publication/ British Library) fire-arms, another way of escape being open, are guilty of murder.' Allen, having arranged the party, given orders and supplied powder and shot, should be regarded as their leader. He pointed out the flaws in John Penny's statement, adding that though he had claimed he could bring witnesses to give him an alibi, none had been brought.

It took the jury only two hours to find all the men guilty, asking for mercy for all except Allen and John Penny. Holroyd said he had no power to remit the sentence of death. To John Penny and Allen he said, 'I can give you no hope in this world.' For the others he would grant a temporary respite and would gladly represent their cases before the Crown.

On 11 April William Adams Brodribb was tried on a charge of administering an unlawful oath, Greenaway being the principal witness against him. Brodribb's ploy of using a book other than the Bible did not assist him, since the men had obviously believed they had sworn on a Testament and that the oath was binding. Brodribb claimed that Greenaway had several times confessed that it was he who had shot Ingram, and accused the servant of self-interest, but the attorney's attempts to wriggle out of the consequences of his actions were not successful: the jury took only two minutes to find him guilty. Holroyd was particularly scathing towards a man who, by his education and profession, ought to have known and acted better. 'You may consider yourself as having been materially instrumental to the fatal consequences which have befallen the eleven unfortunate men, who were yesterday condemned, and who were brought through your means, to consider themselves safe from detection in the perpetration of any outrage, to which they might have been tempted on their expedition.' He sentenced him to the full punishment allowed, which was transportation for seven years.

On 13 April John Allen and John Penny attended chapel for the last time. Just before 1 p.m. they ascended the scaffold together. They briefly addressed the crowds who had come to see them die, both admitting that they had been present at the affray, but both steadfastly claiming their innocence of the actual shooting. After taking their leave of each other they suffered the extreme penalty. They were buried at Thornbury the following day. The other nine men, though sentenced to hang, had been respited until 20 May, and in due course their sentences were reduced to transportation for life. All were sent to Australia. Their fates are unknown.

William Adams Brodribb made a successful new life for himself in Australia. After serving his time he returned to the legal profession and settled in Hobart, where he became clerk to the Judge Advocate, and later served as under-sheriff. His eldest son, also called William Adams Brodribb, enjoyed a most distinguished career, becoming a Justice of the Peace and a member of the Legislative Council of New South Wales.

What became of William Greenaway is not known. If he had had any sense, he would have moved as far as possible from Lower Moreton. He could hardly have been a popular man in the parish of Hill.

4

REVELATIONS

Newent, 1867–72

Shortly after 11 p.m. on 24 February 1867 Mr Edmund Edmonds, a wealthy solicitor of Newent, ran from his house in a state of great agitation to fetch the family doctor. Dr Matthew Bass Smith had already retired for the night, but on being awoken he obligingly rolled out of bed and began to dress. Mrs Ann Edmonds, the solicitor's 51-year-old wife, had, he was told, suffered a fit and was very ill. This was not altogether surprising news, as he had attended to this lady for the last five years: he knew that she had a weak heart and might have an attack at any moment. Mr Edmonds rushed back to his house to check on the condition of his wife but soon returned to Bass Smith's house to find the doctor still dressing. He begged him to hurry and come at once, as he was afraid that his wife was dying.

When Dr Bass Smith arrived he found an anxious tableau in the second-floor bedroom, which was normally shared by the Edmonds's youngest son, 9-year-old Oscar, and Miss Mary Mathews, Mrs Edmonds's younger unmarried sister. Ann Edmonds lay on the floor, pale and unconscious. Trying vainly to revive her were her sister and Jeannette Edmonds, the solicitor's pretty 17-year-old niece, who also resided in the house. Little Oscar had been quickly taken to his father's room after witnessing his mother's collapse.

It must have been more than usually distressing for Dr Bass Smith to see one of his patients in such extremity. In the last five years a friendship had developed between the Smiths and the Edmonds, and in particular a close brotherly regard between the doctor and the solicitor. What Mr Edmonds did not know at the time was that Dr Bass Smith, a 41-year-old married man with four children, had been making unsuccessful attempts to seduce Jeannette.

Bass Smith helped to lift his patient on to the bed and applied the usual remedies of the day. He bled her from the arm and temple, placed croton oil on

| 483 | Twenty fifth February 1867 Pigeon House Newent | Ann Edmonds | | Female | 51 Years | Wife of Edmund Edmonds Solicitor | Apoplexy Certified | M. Bass Smith Present at the death The Villa High Street Newent | Eighth March 1867 | Richard Lovett Burton Registrar | |

Death certificate of Ann Edmonds. (By permission of HMSO)

The tomb of Ann Edmonds. (Author's collection)

her tongue, applied mustard plasters to the back of the neck and hot water to the feet, and gave her an injection, but Mrs Edmonds did not respond. He was told that the collapse had happened without warning and saw no marks of injury on his patient. Despite his best efforts, life ebbed rapidly away, and shortly before 1 a.m. Ann Edmonds breathed her last. The corpse was laid out with care, and Jeannette tenderly arranged her aunt's hair. Dr Bass Smith had no difficulty in signing a death certificate giving the cause of death as apoplexy.

Ann and Edmund had had thirteen children, of whom only four sons were living. The three eldest were not then at home, Edmund jnr being at college in Cambridge and Ralph and Claude at school. There were, however, several servants in the house at the time. Ann Bradd occupied a room on the first-floor landing, and Ann Cassidy was in a room directly above, which she shared with Miss Mesenger, the cook. John Arch, the groom, slept over the stables. In due course every occupant of the house would have a story to tell about the events of that night.

There was a substantial funeral for Mrs Edmonds, as befitted a lady of her position, and the shops in Newent were closed that day as a mark of respect. Edmonds had a heavily ornate white-marble memorial erected on her grave, as an expression of his sad loss. The vicar, the Revd Keene, disapproved of the monument, and from then on he and Edmonds were not on good terms, a matter which did not seem to cause the widower any anxiety.

Life moved on. Miss Mathews took over the duties of managing the household and servants, while Jeannette assisted her uncle by writing letters at his dictation. In May 1867 Ann Bradd quarrelled with Edmonds regarding her failure to fetch some milk. He wanted to dismiss her at once without a 'character' (reference), which would have made it difficult for her to get another situation, but at the request of Miss Mathews she was allowed to stay on, and when she finally left that August, was given good references. Ann Cassidy also left Edmonds's employ, but for quite another reason. She married John Arch, the groom, in November 1867. They went to live in Ashford, Kent, where he became a railway signalman. Miss Mesenger remained with the Edmonds for another four years.

About a year after Mrs Edmonds's death Dr Bass Smith, evidently a patient and persistent gentleman, finally succeeded in making Jeannette Edmonds his mistress. Matters were conducted without the knowledge of her uncle. Even when the doctor left Newent for London, together with his wife and children (now numbering five), the lovers kept in touch. Bass Smith visited his friend on numerous occasions, staying in the house at Newent, but once the family had retired for the night he repaid their hospitality by creeping into Jeannette's room. He took her on holidays to Ross and Kenilworth, where they stayed together at inns, and gave her expensive presents, which had to be carefully explained away. They also exchanged letters, without it coming to the notice of either Edmonds or Mrs Smith, addressing each other affectionately as 'Anthony' and 'Cleopatra'.

In due course Edmund, the eldest son, left Cambridge and went to Australia, Claude became a barrister, while Oscar went to school at Malvern College. Edmonds kept himself busy. He was an exceedingly litigious man and over the years became involved in a great many lawsuits, which he invariably won. His most entrenched opponent was the local squire, Mr Onslow, who suffered substantial financial losses as a result. While there is evidence to suggest that Edmonds had a great many friends, it appears that he was also a man who could easily make enemies. When the Newent Gas Light and Coke Company became bankrupt Edmonds, who was its chairman, was depicted in a satirical poster as the Devil, with miserable shareholders kneeling at his feet.

On 9 October 1871 the settled life of the Edmonds family was to change for ever. Jeannette sat down to write to her 'own dearest Anto', referring to herself as 'your faithful Cleo', but was called away from her desk, leaving the letter only partly completed. This affectionate missive included a shocking indelicacy, for among the chatty family news was the request, 'Have my stays made exactly as you please.' The letter fell into the hands of her uncle, who read the incriminating contents with horror. He approached her with the words, 'You hussy, I've found you out!', slapped her face and ordered her from the house. Jeannette took the very sensible view that her best course of action was to absent herself as soon as possible from her uncle's wrath, with a view to begging his forgiveness once he had cooled down. She was unable to take with her any more than she could carry and was obliged to borrow £1 17s from Ralph Edmonds.

Poster depicting Edmund Edmonds as the Devil after the failure of the gas company. (By kind permission of Dr K.M. Tomlinson)

In 1871 the choices for a young woman who had lost her character and whose relatives could or would not support her were very limited. Jeannette spent a little time with her mother, but evidently this could not continue and she telegraphed to Dr Bass Smith for assistance. He came to collect her and they spent a few days with friends in Gloucestershire before he was obliged to return to London. There Jeannette stayed for a few days with her lover and his family. Dr Bass Smith, presumably finding it inconvenient to have both his wife and his mistress living with him under the same roof, thought it better in the long run that Jeannette go elsewhere. He contacted the Revd Keene for assistance, who came down to London and arranged for Jeannette to enter the St James Diocesan Home in Hammersmith, which she did on 22 October. It was what was then known as a home for fallen women.

And young Jeannette had truly fallen. Now an attractive and prepossessing woman of 22 she had lost a far better position in life than she might ever have expected. Her impecunious father had died in 1859, leaving a widow and seven children. She had been fortunate indeed to have been given a home by her wealthy uncle, who also arranged for her education. Even if she had never attained that ideal of Victorian womanhood – marriage – she was always assured of a home in one of the most luxurious and admired houses in the neighbourhood in return for a few light secretarial duties. She was now penniless, dependent on charity and without a reputation. She was also free from the influence of her uncle.

Bass Smith went to Newent to get Jeannette's boxes for her, but found Edmonds in an implacable mood. He refused to give up the boxes and shook his fist at his erstwhile friend. 'I believe you seduced my niece, you scoundrel!' he exclaimed. 'As long as I have a feather to fly I will have Jeannette!' replied Bass Smith gallantly. 'Then I will take care you will not have her long!' retorted Edmonds.

Bass Smith, gathering that he would not obtain the boxes that day, decided to leave and come back later. Matters were not improved on his second visit. Edmonds's rage was now fully in its stride, and he threatened to have Smith struck off the register of surgeons for his behaviour. The doctor had his own threats to make. He told Edmonds that if the boxes were not given up he would create such a stir in Newent that the dead would rise from the grave. Four months later that was precisely what happened.

Jeannette, meanwhile, had had ample opportunity to ponder her position, and had decided that returning to her enraged and vengeful uncle was her best option. She wrote to him in December 1871 stating that she was very ill, apologising for offending him and asking for his forgiveness. 'The truth is,' she stated, 'my past career is quite bad enough without exaggeration.' It appears that he did not respond; at any rate she remained in the Home.

Edmonds, from what he thought to be a powerful and unassailable position, seemed determined to crush the doctor for his misdeeds. He sued him for a substantial sum of money on the grounds that his charges were excessive, and when Bass Smith was forced to file for bankruptcy to escape the debt, Edmonds appeared at the hearing and successfully halted proceedings. Edmonds also made good his threat of trying to get the doctor struck off the medical register.

Powerless as she appeared, Jeannette did however have one very substantial weapon in her armoury – her knowledge of what had happened on that February night in 1867. It is not known to whom she spoke first, but undoubtedly among those persons who first heard her tale were the Revd Keene and the Lady Superior of the Home. She had, she said, a story to tell which had weighed on her mind for nearly five years, and which she had previously been afraid to tell. It was only now that she was no longer dependent on her uncle for her home and her keep that she was able to reveal the truth. Mrs Edmonds, she said, had not, after all, died a natural death. She had been murdered.

Her uncle and aunt, she said, while outwardly a devoted couple, had in fact had a very unhappy life together. Ann Edmonds was very jealous of her husband's giving professional advice to other ladies, and in the November prior to her death a letter intended for Mr Edmonds had by chance fallen into her hands. The letter was from a woman, and it had been the cause of many quarrels.

On the day of her death Mrs Edmonds had at first appeared to be well and cheerful. The couple had quarrelled in the dining-room at about 7 p.m., but by the time dinner was served they seemed to be reconciled. There had been guests to dinner, a Mr and Mrs Symonds, and Mr Palmer, Edmonds's articled clerk. Everyone had had a very pleasant evening. Jeannette and her aunt had sung a duet for the company, a song entitled 'Too Late, Too Late', which had been very well received. Ann Bradd had waited at table. Conversation during dinner was on a number of topics, among which was Miss Smallridge, a young lady of their acquaintance who lived at Gloucester and whose beauty had been praised. The guests went home, and at 10.30 p.m. Jeannette, Miss Mathews and the servants retired for the night, little Oscar having been put to bed rather earlier.

Shortly before 11 p.m. Jeannette heard her aunt and uncle quarrelling again, and then came a scream. She got out of bed and went downstairs. She saw her aunt come out of the dining-room and rush upstairs, greatly distressed. Ann Edmonds, a bedroom candlestick in her hand, had hurried up to Miss Mathews's room, where that lady and young Oscar were in their respective beds. Trembling with agitation, she placed the candlestick on the dressing table. Edmonds burst into the room in a great rage, threatening to sell up his home and go away. His wife fled from him to the other side of Oscar's bed and crouched down. In great distress she said, two or three times, 'Jeannette, I am dying!'

'You be damned!' Edmonds exclaimed, to which she retorted that she would not be damned. Then he rushed across the room and struck her on the side of the head with his clenched fist. Weakly, Ann Edmonds asked Jeannette to bring her some water, then sank down on to a box beside the bed. Jeannette brought the water,

Nicholson House, the former magistrate's court, Newent. (Author's collection)

and her aunt drank some of it, but then her head drooped to one side. Jeannette tried to undo her aunt's dress to make her more comfortable, but her body seemed to be swelling and so she could not. As she tended to the stricken woman, her aunt raised her hand weakly to the side of her head two or three times where she had received the blow, but she never spoke again. At one point Jeannette thought Edmonds would strike his wife again; she did her best to protect her but was pushed to one side. By now, however, Miss Mathews was out of bed and helped to lay the sick woman on the floor. Ann Bradd had also been roused from her bed by the commotion and was sent down to the kitchen to make some gruel. Jeannette went to get some restoratives, and Edmonds rushed out to get the doctor. Jeannette believed that her uncle had struck his wife downstairs with the clothes brush that usually hung in the hall. She had seen the brush on the following day, and the handle had been broken off. She also thought that he had thrown a candlestick at her aunt, as one of the bedroom candlesticks was later found to be bent, and there was candle grease on Mrs Edmonds's dress. Jeannette's listeners were no doubt shocked to hear this story but agreed that the matter could not be allowed to rest any longer. The coroner would have to be informed.

The coroner for the Western Division of Gloucestershire was a Mr Carter, who at once took it upon himself to visit Jeannette and take her statement. It so happened that Carter had his own very peculiar and personal reasons for taking an interest in this case. In 1855 he had been one of the parties interested in the Chancery suit of *Edmonds* v. *Legge*, an action arising from the most scandalous of circumstances.

In the early 1840s a young Edmund Edmonds arrived in Newent and became articled clerk to a solicitor, Mr Cadle, who had then lived in the very house that Edmonds later owned, the curiously named Pigeon House in the High Street. Edmonds had become acquainted with a married couple, Richard and Ann Legge, and it seemed that the young man was a great favourite with them both. Mr Legge, however, was a man of intemperate habits – in other words, he drank. One night in November 1843 he was brought home ignominiously in his own gig, having suffered an attack of paralysis. Although he slowly recovered sufficiently to be able to move around on crutches, he remained paralysed down one side of his body and was never again the man he had been; indeed, he confided to his doctor that he was no longer able to perform the duties of his marital bed. The Legges, who had married in 1835, had had one child in 1837, who died, but in the spring of 1844 Mrs Legge again found herself to be pregnant. There had for some time been suspicions in the town of an immoral connection between the married lady and the clerk, who was three years her junior. These suspicions were confirmed when a servant happened to see something not intended for her eyes and reported the scandal. The unfortunate Mrs Legge was mobbed in the streets, and the whole matter led to public disturbances such that the Superintendent of Police was called away from Gloucester on more than one occasion to quell the disorder. It was even said, though later denied, that the lady had been burned in effigy.

Model of Pigeon House used at the trial of Edmund Edmonds in 1872. (By kind permission of Dr K.M. Tomlinson)

Mrs Legge had been indiscreet enough to write some letters to Mr Edmonds, the terms of which left it in no doubt that the two had an adulterous relationship. She also expressed the belief that the child she carried was not her husband's but that of her lover. Somehow these letters went astray. They never reached Mr Edmonds but fell into the hands of a Dr Hollister, who had once quarrelled with the young clerk. Dr Hollister, however, did nothing with the letters; he simply put them away for such a time as they might prove useful. In February 1844 Mr Legge suffered another stroke and in June, aged just 35, he died. The following October the widow Legge was delivered of an infant daughter, Mary Frances.

In October 1845 Edmund Edmonds and Mrs Ann Legge were married and became legal guardians of the child. As the daughter of the late Mr Legge, Mary Frances was heir to a sum of £5,500 (about £310,000 nowadays), but when, sadly, little Mary Frances passed away in 1849 Mrs Edmonds became entitled to the money. Since she was a married woman the sum effectively became the property of Edmund Edmonds. This was the moment when Dr Hollister chose to reveal the existence of the incriminating letters. The Legge family brought an action to prove that the child was the daughter not of Mr Legge but of Edmund Edmonds, for if Mary Frances was illegitimate, then, they hoped, the legacy would revert to the Legge family coffers. The case came to court in 1855, and while it was not disputed that the letters were genuine, the courts held that a mother could not legally bastardise her own issue, since, as a matter of policy and morality, it was not permissible for the secrets of the marriage chamber to be publicly disclosed. The case was thus decided in favour of Mr and Mrs Edmonds. Seventeen years later it probably still rankled.

One question Mr Carter must no doubt have asked Jeannette was why Miss Mathews and little Oscar had said nothing about the circumstances of the fatal night. Jeannette pointed out that both were under the influence of Mr Edmonds and would therefore say whatever he told them to say – it was only after she had left the house that she herself had felt able to speak. She also hinted that in Miss Mathews's case there was another more shocking reason for her silence. The relationship between Mr Edmonds and his wife's sister had been more intimate than might have been considered appropriate. Indeed, said Jeannette, Miss Mathews had once suffered a miscarriage. Carter, with the case of *Edmonds* v. *Legge* still burning freshly in his mind, must have found that very believable. He applied to the Secretary of State for an order to exhume the corpse of Mrs Edmonds.

On Tuesday 13 February 1872 the costly marble monument over the grave of Mrs Edmonds was dismantled. The coffin was lifted, carried into the church and opened. Several medical men examined the remains, but they were so decomposed that it was impossible to say how death had occurred. All they could say was that the skull had not been fractured, but given Mrs Edmonds's delicate state of health, it would not have required a heavy blow to kill her.

On the following day Carter presided over the first official inquiry into the death of Mrs Ann Edmonds, which was held at the George Hotel, Newent. Edmonds attended voluntarily, sitting beside his legal advisor and prompting him from time to time. The first person to give evidence was Ann Bradd, a lady of whom it must be said that, whatever she had to tell, she felt it would always be improved by dramatic embellishment. Miss Bradd had been in her bedroom, but still awake, at 11 p.m., and on hearing the noise of the quarrel downstairs she had crept out of her room to see what was happening. She had heard the sound of blows in the dining-room, and Mrs Edmonds had cried out as if being struck before she fled from the room, screaming terribly as she ran up the stairs from her enraged husband. Bradd said she had seen Mrs Edmonds run into her sister's bedroom, where her husband swore at her and struck her a blow on the head. Later, while in the ground-floor kitchen, she had heard the poor woman's death rattle, which was so loud it had sounded through the house. The following morning a broken clothes brush was found in the dining-room. This item had usually hung in the hallway, and Bradd thought that it was with this that the blows downstairs had been delivered. As the inquest was adjourned to the next day Mr Edmonds, protesting loudly and indignantly, was arrested on a charge of murder.

On 15 February the chief witness was Jeannette, who, impressing the court with her cool assurance, repeated what she had said in her original statement. She admitted the intimacy with Dr Bass Smith, which caused some sensation among the listening public. When charged with her long silence on the circumstances of her aunt's death, she said that she had discussed it with Miss Mathews and with Bass Smith, but was afraid to take the matter further while still living with her uncle. She was shocked and disgusted at his behaviour, but had never spoken to him about it.

Ann Bradd, recalled to the stand, gave further details of the quarrel in the dining-room. Mrs Edmonds had called her husband a brute and a wretch, and accused him of going to see another lady in Gloucester. He had said, 'Damn your eyes, go to bed!' and flung something at her. The unfortunate lady cried out, 'Don't, dear man!' and ran screaming from the room. When Mrs Edmonds had run into her sister's room Miss Bradd had gone to the door, which was ajar, and from there witnessed the whole scene as described by Jeannette. She said she had told the other servants what had happened but was advised by them to keep quiet. Her opinion was that Mrs Edmonds had been killed by the blow on the head. She had, she said, often heard Mr Edmonds swear at his wife and say he wished she was dead.

Dr Bass Smith gave evidence that Mrs Edmonds suffered from a weak heart and a congested liver. A month before her death he had attended her for bleeding at the nose. At the time of her death he had felt justified in certifying the cause as apoplexy. He had later urged Jeannette to make her statement public, but she did not wish to while she was under the controlling influence of her uncle. Smith claimed that at the funeral the grieving Mr Edmonds had said, 'I feel that I have murdered my wife owing to my unkindness towards her. I wish I could see my time over again, I would behave very differently toward her, for she was indeed a good woman.' The medical witnesses were unable to say if any violence had been used against Mrs Edmonds. While there was nothing to suggest that apoplexy was not the cause of death, it might have been caused by a blow or it might have been brought on by excitement or running upstairs.

Edmonds said in evidence that his wife's health had been breaking down for a number of years. He denied absolutely that any quarrel had taken place. He had never sworn at his wife or used violence towards her, and he had not had any improper relationship with Miss Mathews. He also totally denied that he had had improper intercourse with his wife before they were married. He accused Dr Bass Smith of instigating the inquiry because he had once sued him.

The three other servants who had been in the house on the fatal night, Ann Arch (née Cassidy), her husband John and Mary Mesenger, had been brought from their respective homes to give evidence at the inquest on Mr Edmonds's behalf. All three stayed as guests at Edmonds's house for several days, taking their meals there, and no doubt had ample opportunity to discuss the case with the family. On the last day of the inquiry the dinner guests, Mr and Mrs Symonds, Ralph Edmonds and the servants all gave evidence that Edmonds had always been kind to his wife. Fourteen-year-old Oscar, who had been brought from school to attend the hearing, said he was sure his father did not strike his mother.

The jury deliberated, and in this they had not a little assistance from Mr Carter, who made sure they were acquainted with the circumstances of *Edmonds* v. *Legge*. Despite protests from Edmonds and his counsel, Carter read to them

The churchyard of St Mary's, Newent. (Author's collection)

portions of the Law Society report on that case. They returned a verdict that Mrs Edmonds died from apoplexy, and that her death was accelerated by violence. Edmonds was committed for trial on a charge of manslaughter. A few days later he appeared before the magistrate. If he had hoped for better luck in that court, he was to be disappointed, for the magistrate in question was none other than his old adversary Squire Onslow, who, with enormous satisfaction, committed him for trial at Gloucester Assizes on a charge of wilful murder.

Between the inquiry and the trial there was a rather unusual occurrence. The Revd Keene, Vicar of Newent, preached a special sermon in which he took as his subject the recent inquiry. It was an action he was later to regret. Keene, deeply moved during the delivery of the discourse, pointed out how Daniel had felt when the sins of the people came home to him. This, he said, was the feeling a Christian should have – pain, grief and shame at the notion of sin – after the awful revelations of wickedness among themselves, now blazing forth to all the world. The sermon was later printed and distributed for the edification of the public.

To add to the family's tragedies, on 21 February James Mathews, the brother of Mrs Edmonds, tried to commit suicide by cutting his throat. He survived and was taken to the County Asylum. He had been in business as a farmer and maltster but had lately fallen on hard times. It was possible that the recent scandal had added to his woes and precipitated the attempt. The local newspapers seized upon the shocking circumstances with great glee, and repeated every juicy detail of the gossip that was rife in the town. 'The career of the chief actor is one of unblushing immorality!' enthused the *Western Mail*. The *Ross Gazette* copied the article, and the *Gloucester Mercury* joined in the exposé.

The *Gloucester Journal* displayed placards headed 'Wife murder by a solicitor!' with the preceding words 'Charge of' in rather smaller lettering. It was rumoured that the proprietor had told a newsvendor that there was no doubt of Edmonds's guilt, and that he would hang as he deserved. 'Listen to what is said of the last moments of the inhabitant of this silent tomb,' emoted the leader. 'Hear and compare that foul story with the pure whiteness of the costly marble monument. Lift the blinds of yonder house, the seeming abode of white-winged peace. But shrink away in horror at the cry that comes through the open casement. Lust, unholy passion, strife, anguish and then a charge of murder.' The writer then added that he could say no more about the case as it had not yet been tried. He had already said far too much.

Unusually, Edmonds was granted bail – although at the personal security of £4,000, a not inconsiderable sum. He then brought an application to have the case removed to London on the grounds that it was impossible to have a fair trial in Gloucester. The application was made under what was known as the Palmer Act, which had been passed to enable the trial of William Palmer to be removed from Rugeley because of local prejudice. (It did not assist Palmer, who was hanged.)

Edmonds drew the judge's attention to the reports in the local newspapers and also the sermon preached by his 'enemy' the Revd Keene, a copy of which was submitted for consideration. He complained about unfairness by his 'enemy' the Coroner in raking up the old case of *Edmonds* v. *Legge*, which had been brought by the malice of his 'enemy' Dr Hollister; he complained about the unfairness of his appearing before his 'enemy' Mr Onslow; he complained about the local prejudice against him which had led to the composition and circulation of some lines of doggerel. If there had been heard a fluttering noise in court, it could well have been the sound of a great many chickens coming home to roost. After four days of hearings it was agreed that the case could be transferred to London.

On 5 April the indictment was heard at Gloucester Crown Court. Mr Baron Cleasby pointed out to the jury the difference in law between murder and manslaughter. This was given careful consideration, and when the jury returned from their deliberations the clerk read out their conclusions amid a breathless silence in the courtroom. They had found a true bill against Edmonds, but on the charge of manslaughter.

The trial opened on 8 May, when Edmonds pleaded not guilty. After the opening address he made an application to leave the dock and sit at the solicitors' table to be able to communicate better with his counsel. Mr Baron Bramwell, presiding, allowed this privilege with some misgivings, saying it was unusual, though not unprecedented. He supposed every prisoner would like to be able to sit near his counsel if he had the option.

The first witness for the prosecution was Ann Bradd. She again described the terrible quarrel, how Edmonds had banged the door of his office, the sound of a heavy object being thrown and the dreadful screams of Mrs Edmonds as she fled upstairs. She believed that the missile was a candlestick. She said she had told both Ann Cassidy and John Arch about what she had seen but had been advised

Stardens, the home of the Onslow family. (Contemporary postcard)

to say nothing. Before she left she had told Edmonds that he was a bad man and bad would be his end. She continued to maintain that while in the kitchen she had heard the death rattle of the lady on the second floor. By now Ann Bradd was getting thoroughly into her role as witness, and she claimed that since leaving the Edmonds's service she had had many good places but had always left them because she had been haunted by Mrs Edmonds. On being pressed by an incredulous counsel, even Ann Bradd realised that her imagination had overstepped the mark, and she said that what had haunted her was the memory of what she had seen and heard. She added she had previously been pressed by Mrs Edmonds's mother to tell everything she knew, and that it would be hundreds of pounds in her pocket if she would tell what happened that night. Virtuously, Ann Bradd declared that she would not be bribed, and she had in any event already promised Miss Mathews that she would say nothing.

Jeannette repeated her evidence but now claimed that she had not left her uncle's house on account of her relationship with Dr Bass Smith. Instead, she said she had made an error copying out some correspondence for her uncle and he had struck her on the head, and it was because of that she had left. She was tasked with the contents of a letter she had written to her mother on 11 March 1867, in which she described her aunt's death as due to apoplexy, but Jeannette stated that she had written only what she had been told to write by Miss Mathews.

Mr Huddleston, counsel for the defence, addressed the jury. He taunted Dr Bass Smith, accusing him of having concocted the entire story after Edmonds had taken action against him. 'None are more vindictive than those who had wronged others,' he stated. The story of Miss Mathews's intimacy with Mr Edmonds he said had also been concocted to destroy her credibility. It was, he believed, no coincidence that the tale had emerged in January, when all London had been reading in the newspapers about a trial for wife-murder.

Miss Mathews was now called to give her evidence. She described Edmonds as a 'generous, kind and affectionate husband'. That evening in February 1867 the supper had gone pleasantly, no lady had been praised for her beauty and there had been no quarrel and no screams. When Mrs Edmonds had come into the room to say goodnight, as was her habit, she was calm and quiet and spoke as usual. Mr Edmonds was intending to go to London the next day but his wife had tried to dissuade him, as she was unwell. There was normal, quiet conversation. Then, suddenly, Ann Edmonds asked for some water. Once she had drunk some she said that she felt ill and was dying, and sank back on a box by the bed. Mr Edmonds had not struck his wife or sworn at her. Miss Mathews had not told anyone to be silent about any blow. She recalled the brush referred to, but it had not been found broken the next morning. She denied absolutely that any impropriety had passed between herself and Mr Edmonds.

Oscar gave evidence and was adamant that his father had not struck his mother. He remembered the incident perfectly, and though he had of course discussed it with his father, he denied that he had been coached by him as to what to say.

Ann Arch said that although she was in bed at the time of Mrs Edmonds's death she was still awake and had heard no screams. She denied that Ann Bradd had told her about a blow and a quarrel. She too thought that the brush was still whole after that night. Questioned about the bedroom candlesticks, she said that they were always left on a hall table downstairs in the evening, together with a lamp and some tapers, so each individual would light their own candle before going upstairs. John Arch then testified that he had heard nothing untoward that night, and that Ann Bradd had said nothing unusual to him the following day. He thought that the clothes brush had not been broken the day after Mrs Edmonds's death.

Mrs Symonds, the dinner guest, had been a governess with the family for eleven years and testified that Mr and Mrs Edmonds had always been on good terms. She had noticed a bent candlestick but had thought the candle grease on Mrs Edmonds's dress had been caused by her accidentally sitting down near to a greasy candlestick.

Ralph Edmonds had been at school at the time of his mother's death, but in October 1871 he had been in the office and heard heated words between his father and Jeannette when the letter to Dr Bass Smith had been found. He described the blow his father had delivered as a slight tap on the face, after Jeannette had looked at him in 'a saucy way'.

Finally there was a new witness: Miss Mary Edmonds, Jeannette's sister. She testified that her uncle had assisted all the family after her father had died. She had visited the house in the September following her aunt's death, and the clothes brush had been whole on her arrival. She herself had seen it accidentally broken by her cousin Edmund while he was romping in the hallway.

Ann Bradd's claim to have heard the death rattle was countered by the production of a large wooden model of the house, which clearly demonstrated the substantial distance between the kitchen and the upper bedroom.

Baron Bramwell summed up. If the deceased had really received a blow on the head, then it was a legitimate conclusion that this had killed her. But where, he asked, was the evidence of the blow? Ann Bradd had supported Jeannette's story but was contradicted by all the other witnesses as to the screams she said she had heard. The brush, which was said to have been broken in February, was not broken until many months later. There was also the unusual incident of the bedroom candle. Everyone agreed that Mrs Edmonds had arrived in the second-floor bedroom with a lighted candle. Evidence had been given that these were placed on a hall table unlit for each person to light their own. The court was being asked to believe that when Mrs Edmonds had fled from her husband in terror, she had paused by the hall table to light a candle. When people came up with a story many years after an event it was vital to ask why, and both Dr Bass Smith and Jeannette had motives for revenge against Mr Edmonds. No one, he said, could fail to perceive that the case had its origin in some very devilish source.

The jury retired and, after deliberating for less than fifteen minutes, returned a verdict of not guilty. Edmonds was released.

The Holts, Newent. (Contemporary postcard)

The slab under which the ashes of Edmund Edmonds are said to be buried. (Author's collection)

Of course it could not end there. Hell hath no fury like a solicitor libelled. Edmonds brought civil actions for libel against the proprietors and publishers of the *Western Mail,* the *Ross Gazette,* the *Gloucester Mercury* and the *Gloucester Journal* – and of course the Revd Keene. There was also the matter of the slanderous comment to the newsvendor. The defendants, like vultures who had descended on a body only to find it alive and kicking, whined that they had no malice against the plaintiff and could not in any case afford to pay substantial damages. The courts suggested that the two sides try to reach an amicable settlement, but Edmonds was having none of it. He pressed on to the bitter end.

The libels were proved, though not the slander, as the newsvendor concerned had a curious lapse of memory about the conversation. Edmonds was awarded damages of £350 from the *Journal,* £350 from the *Mercury,* £1,000 from the *Mail,* and only 40s (£2) from the *Gazette,* which had published a retraction and apology. The Revd Keene was ordered to pay £400.

No action for perjury seems to have been taken against Bass Smith, Jeannette or Ann Bradd. The motive of the first two was obvious, but a clue to that of Ann Bradd may be detected in her evidence at the trial.

Edmonds's triumph was short-lived. His practice suffered, and by 1881 his handsome house (renamed the Holts) was sold, and he filed for bankruptcy. The man who had generously given homes to nieces and nephews was obliged to live as a boarder in the London home of the ever-faithful Miss Mathews. It is not known where or when he died, as no certificate can be traced, but in Newent it is believed that he died in a workhouse. Behind the ornate tomb of his wife there is a plain, square slab with a Latin inscription which states that the ashes of Edmund Edmonds have been placed beneath. The Holts was demolished in the 1950s to make way for a new health centre.

In 1873 Dr Matthew Bass Smith was struck off the medical register for 'infamous professional conduct' but was restored in 1884. He established a medical practice in London, but separated from his wife, though his children remained with him. He died in 1895.

Jeannette married in 1885. Her husband was George Thomson, a 43-year-old steward at Croydon Infirmary, who was a widower with three children. Their son, Gilbert, was born the following year. It is to be hoped that Jeannette's lively imagination was restricted thereafter to the telling of bedtime stories.

5
TRIPLE EVENT

Arlingham, Stapleton and Gloucester, 1873–4

On 12 January 1874 the city of Gloucester was preparing for a rare event: the simultaneous hanging of three people within the walls of its jail. Two murders had been committed on the same day, yet the nature of the two crimes and the character of those doomed to suffer the extreme penalty were so very different that many people were led to question the existence of a punishment that could sweep away both the irredeemably wicked and the victim of passionate despair.

In 1870 Amelia Selina Phipps, then 20 years of age, whose father Edwin was a farmer at Paganhill near Stroud, went to live with her brother Thomas as housekeeper of West End Farm at Arlingham. Arlingham is situated on marshy ground about a mile from the eastern shore of the River Severn, which surrounds it on three sides. Nearby St Augustine's Farm was occupied by James Merrett, husband of Amelia's older sister Charlotte, and some 200 yards away was Church Farm, whose tenant was Ellen Butt, a widow with twelve children. Her eldest son had gone to America, and next in age was Charles Edward (usually called Edward), a year younger than Amelia, who had taken on many of the duties of running the farm and caring for the huge household. He was trustworthy, hard-working and a good farmer, and was godfather to one of James Merrett's children.

His downfall was his all-consuming passion for Amelia. She was a friendly and outgoing young woman, and had, probably unintentionally, given Edward the impression that her regard was more than just friendship. When he made his feelings known, she told him firmly but kindly that any closer connection was out of the question. Perhaps she simply did not find him attractive. He was about 5ft 3in in height, slightly built with dark hair and whiskers and a low, receding forehead, although it was said that his face was not unpleasant, and he dressed in smart, well-fitting clothing. The close proximity of the families, and the old ties of friendship which meant they called on each other frequently, meant that Edward saw Amelia often, and as time went on his frustration turned into anger. Amelia was happy to spend time with him socially, but she was also on friendly terms with other young men, which fuelled his jealousy. Although there was no engagement between them he felt that her friendliness with others was tantamount to unfaithfulness to him. On 11 August 1873 there was a country

West End Farm. (Author's collection)

feast at Longney, with dancing all night, and Amelia and Edward went there together. The pleasurable evening deteriorated into a violent quarrel. Edward reproached Amelia for dancing with other men, to which she replied that it was very improper to dance only with one. Edward, who was a little the worse for drink, became increasingly miserable, and on the way home there was a renewed confrontation, during which he hit Amelia, giving her a black eye. She must have retaliated, for afterwards it was seen that Edward was sporting a bruised face and a scratch on his nose. After that, despite his tears and apologies, Amelia's manner towards him was distinctly cold. She refused to tell how she had come by the black eye, but to her relatives it was obvious what had happened.

On the following Saturday there was a visitor to West End Farm: Harry Goddard, a farmer from Frocester. Goddard was 29 years old and single. The plan was for him to stay there for three nights, since the Arlingham feast was to take place on the following day. That Sunday Edward visited West End Farm, where Amelia was busy preparing dinner. He helped her with the beans, but she made it obvious that she had not asked him to do so and in fact didn't want his help. By contrast, her manner towards Harry Goddard was friendly and playful, and she once or twice tugged his hair teasingly to get his attention. There were a number of others there that day on account of the forthcoming feast, including James Merrett and a cousin, Richard Hill. After dinner they went to church, Amelia wearing a white dress and walking arm in arm with her cousin. They passed the Butts' farm on the way, where Edward, standing at the gate, saw them go by. On their return from church the whole party collected at West End Farm

St Augustine's Farm, Arlingham. (Author's collection)

for tea and afterwards went to Merrett's house. Harry Goddard and Amelia went out into the garden, and Edward, who had joined the party, followed them. There was talk of the forthcoming Gloucester cheese fair on the Monday, Harry suggesting that if Amelia and James were going he could drive them. To this, Amelia agreed.

When Amelia walked back to West End Farm she went arm in arm with Edward, who repeatedly asked her to go to the cheese fair with him, but she said no, she had already promised Mr Goddard. They reached West End Farm at about 8.15 p.m. Shortly before 9 p.m. some of the party returned home, Amelia, James Merrett and Edward remaining. Thomas Phipps went out into the road to bid farewell to his guests, together with Harry Goddard. They did not return immediately, and meanwhile James Merrett leaned on the front gate looking out at the road while Amelia and Edward were walking and talking on the lawn outside the house. Amelia suddenly called out 'James! James!' He turned and hurried over to her. 'This fellow is going to murder me, is going to stab me with his knife,' she said.

'Whatever are you thinking about?' said James to Edward. 'Why do you make yourself so foolish?' 'You have deceived me, Amelia,' Edward protested, to which she replied, 'I have told you scores of times I should never have you.'

Edward again said he wanted her to go with him to Gloucester the following day, but again she refused, saying she was going with James and Mr Goddard. 'There'll be something bad the matter,' said Edward, ominously. Once more he asked her. Once more she refused.

James pointed out to Edward that it was hardly likely she would trust herself with him after the way he had ill-treated her coming home from the Longney feast. This was a perfectly reasonable comment, but Edward did not seem to be amenable to reason. All three then went into the house, where James sat Edward down and had a good talk to him, saying that he had a kind mother and sisters, a good farm well stocked and everything to make him happy and comfortable. These soothing words seemed to have no effect. Yet again Edward asked Amelia to go with him to Gloucester, and again she said she would not. 'I'll do as I told, I'll be damned if I don't,' he exclaimed, repeating the words several times, and raising and lowering his arm in a stabbing motion. Jumping up, he took Amelia's arm, saying, 'Come with me, Amelia,' and they both went out to the lawn, James following. They all went to the gate together, and as Merrett stood listening to some voices from up the road, Edward took Amelia's arm and drew her away until they were standing some 4 yards from the front door of the house. He started to upbraid her again about her friendliness towards other men. 'I don't like one more than another, Edward,' said Amelia. 'I shall talk to anyone.'

It was dark, so when Merrett, hearing the report of a gun behind him, turned around and looked, he could not at first see anything. There was a wall at the end of the house, on the other side of which was a field in which there was a hedge and, beyond that, the River Severn. He distinctly heard the sound of someone forcing a way through the hedge and ran to where Amelia had been standing. Making her out in the gloom by her white dress, he found her lying on the ground, her body thrashing convulsively. She had been hit with the full force of a single-barrelled shotgun, which had torn into her neck just below the left ear, blown away most of her lower jaw and destroyed the major blood vessels of the neck. Some shot was lodged in her fingers where she had raised her hand to protect herself. There was no doctor in the village, so Dr Morris of Frampton-on-Severn was sent for, but recovery from such a wound was impossible. Amelia was dead in a few minutes.

A single-barrelled shotgun was found lying on the lawn near where Amelia had fallen, and it was quickly identified as Edward's. It later transpired that some half an hour before the murder he had rushed back home for his gun, returning quickly to place it on the lawn by the parlour window, where it lay unseen in the darkness. Of Edward there was no trace, and it appeared that after committing the murder he had headed towards the River Severn. At the inquest on Amelia, which took place at the Red Lion Inn, Arlingham, the coroner, Mr Ball, observed that 'all of them knew what running towards a river under such circumstances generally meant'. Searches were made but no trace of Edward's body could be found. On 23 August 1873 Amelia Selina Phipps was buried in the graveyard at Whiteshill Church, half a mile from her parents' farm at Paganhill.

On the very same day that Edward Butt shot Amelia Phipps another murder took place of a very different character. While Edward had acted in the hot blood of an obsession, what came to be known as the Horfield poisoning was cold, calculated and cruel.

On 23 October 1872, 17-year-old Mary Susan Jenkins (usually called Susan) gave birth to a daughter, Sarah. Susan was unmarried, and declared that the

James Merrett.
(Collection of Robert
and Elaine Jewell)

father of her child was 31-year-old Edwin Bailey, who kept a boot and shoe shop
at Boyce's Avenue, Clifton. Bailey, the illegitimate son of a hat clipper's daughter
from Winterbourne, had a long history of misconduct with women. He had
previously worked for a Mr Harry Jacobs in Westgate Street, Gloucester, and
while there had paid his addresses to a young lady. Her policeman father made
enquiries and discovered that the suitor was not, as he had claimed, a single man,
but had a wife who was an invalid and lived in London. Bailey made a hurried
departure and set up a business in Clifton. Young women could rarely enter his
shop without danger of molestation, and many servant girls having once been
sent there on an errand refused ever to go there again. Susan had been in service
with a lady at Clifton who had sent her to the shop to get some boots repaired.
Bailey, said Susan, had dragged her into an inner room and there assaulted her,
cramming a handkerchief into her mouth to stifle her cries. Susan did not report
the incident. Indeed, she later returned to the shop, where further intimacies took
place, resulting in pregnancy. When the baby was born Bailey vehemently denied

Amelia Selina Phipps. (Collection of Robert
and Elaine Jewell)

responsibility to anyone who
would listen and refused to
pay maintenance. What Susan
may not have known at the
time was that Bailey was
already making payments
on another paternity suit.
Susan was obliged to
obtain an affiliation order,
which required the
reluctant father to pay her
5s (25p) a week until the
child was 16, and the costs
of the confinement. Grudg-
ingly, he complied.

Susan had returned to live
with her parents, Elizabeth
and James Jenkins, and her two
brothers and sister, at Myrtle
Cottage, Stapleton, which was next
door to a public house called the
Volunteer Inn. Stapleton was then a
village, considered to be a suburb of Bristol,
some 2 miles north-east of the city. It lay adjacent
to the agricultural village of Horfield, to which it was linked by Gloucester Road,
and was near to the suburbs of Cotham and Clifton. The cottage was shared with
another family, the Fullers. Here Susan received the maintenance money, which
was paid through a local policeman called Constable Critchley. In December
1872 Susan was obliged to go back into service at Cheltenham Road, Clifton,
leaving the child with her mother.

Shortly before Christmas Mrs Jenkins received a visitor, a lady who was a
stranger to her. She was about 30 years of age and gave her name as Anne, but
was curiously reticent about her surname. Anne asked if Mrs Jenkins had a
daughter who was a dressmaker, as her sister would like to have a dress made,
and promised to call another day with the material. The baby was in its
grandmother's lap, and Anne, asking Elizabeth whether it was her daughter's
child, exclaimed that little Sarah was very like a child she had lost, and, weeping,
begged a lock of her hair. She said she had lost the lock of hair from her own
child, and her husband had ill-used her as a consequence. From that time on
Anne visited Mrs Jenkins once or twice a week and took tea with the family. At

MURDER IN GLOUCESTERSHIRE

The shooting of Amelia Selina Phipps. (Illustrated Police News, 1873)

first, Anne said that she lived in Paul Street, Kingsdown, Bristol, but later gave her address as St James Barton. She said that she did needlework, which was curious in view of her initial enquiry for someone to make a dress. Her husband, she said, was called 'Louis'. Later Susan thought Anne had said he was a gentleman clerk in Broad Street, but Elizabeth believed he was a porter. Either way, he was working for only 15s (75p) a week, and when Elizabeth commented that this was a low wage Anne said he was working to redeem his character, which suggested that he had previously lost his character (or good reputation) for some reason she would not mention. Mrs Jenkins was later unsure of Anne's sister's name but thought it was either Nelmes or Elms.

Just after Christmas Susan visited her mother with some good news and met Anne for the first time. A household such as the Jenkins family often had to rely on the charity of kind ladies for little extras for their children, and Susan mentioned that her employer, Mrs Jarvis, was going to talk to a lady at Cotham on her behalf. At once Anne said, 'I suppose you mean the Dorcas Society.' The Jenkinses had never heard of the Dorcas Society (a Christian women's charitable organisation which provided clothing for the poor), which Anne said had taken an interest in little Sarah. Time passed, but nothing was heard from the Dorcas

Society or the lady at Cotham. Anne seemed to have forgotten about the dress that was to be made for her sister, so eventually Mrs Jenkins asked where the material was. Anne said her sister had broken her spine in an accident and was in the Infirmary, so would not after all want the dress made. The visits continued, Anne making a fuss over little Sarah who reminded her so much of her own lost child, and bringing small gifts such as sponge cakes and socks, or giving pennies to Susan's 9-year-old sister. Told that the father of Susan's child was Edwin Bailey, Anne said she didn't know him or where he lived, but declared that he must be a great blackguard. Only the last part of this statement was correct. Anne knew exactly where Edwin Bailey lived because she was employed by him. Quite what the relationship was between the two was never established. It has often been suggested that she was his common-law wife; however, the only evidence on the subject was from an employee of Bailey's, who said that Anne was simply a charwoman who cleaned the shop.

In May 1873 Anne asked Susan whether she had heard from the Dorcas Society. Susan said she had not and supposed that the lady had forgotten about her. 'Oh no,' said Anne, 'ladies often take a time before they send or give; you may find a friend there yet.' Anne would often nurse the child, but when she asked whether she could take it out, Susan would not permit it. She never explained her reason for this reluctance, but perhaps she was suspicious of Anne's excessive affection, fearing she might take the child and not bring it back. When

Whiteshill church. (Author's collection)

Susan moved to another employment at Berkeley Road, Horfield, Anne asked whether she might adopt the child, but Susan said that her mother would care for it. Sarah was a healthy child with no more than the usual minor ailments, but in the summer of 1873 she was teething and sometimes fretful. That June Anne asked Mrs Jenkins what medicine she gave the baby, and on being told magnesia (a common antacid and mild laxative), she recommended Steedman's Soothing Powders as more beneficial. Mrs Jenkins had heard of them but said she had never seen or used one, as they were very expensive. Anne continued to recommend Steedman's powders and asked if there was a visitor who could get her some, but Mrs Jenkins said there wasn't.

In August 1873 Bailey's paternity payments fell three weeks into arrears. The affiliation order still irked him, and he talked of making an appeal. Angrily, he said that he would like to hear that the child had died and would give half a sovereign (50p) to anyone who would bring him news of its death. Constable Critchley went to see Bailey about the arrears. There had been some suggestion that Bailey was to give Susan £100 to settle the matter, something he indignantly denied. He told Critchley he would not give her £100, nor £50, nor £5 to settle it, and if he could get witnesses he would take the matter to a higher court.

On 13 August Anne again asked if anything had come from the Dorcas Society. Susan had no more hopes of any assistance from that quarter, but Anne said she could depend upon it: she would receive something soon. On that day a letter arrived, addressed to 'Susan Jenkins, near the Volunteer Public House, Horfield, near Bristol'. Inside were three small packets labelled 'Steedman's Soothing Powders', and a shilling's (5p) worth of stamps. The enclosed note stated that the items came 'From a lady visitor of Cotham Dorcas Society, who will send a few things for the child to wear in a day or two'. It included instructions on how to give the powders. The letter was signed 'Jane Isabella Smith, Hope Cottage, Cotham'. Susan asked James Fuller to write a thank-you note, which went:

> Madam, I received your kind letter, and I return you many thanks for your kind present, which I was badly in want of, as I have not been able to earn much myself, which makes us very short at present. I remain your humble servant, S Jenkins.

On the following day the note was returned undelivered to the Dead Letter Office, but it was not sent back to Susan until several days later. When Anne called again on 14 August she asked how the child was and was told it was teething. Susan said that the expected letter had been received, and Anne enquired whether the child had been given one of the powders. On being told no, she replied, 'I wish you would, as they do children so much good when they are teething.' Mrs Jenkins thought that Anne was low in spirits that day and had been crying. Anne explained that she would not be able to call to see them again, as her husband was removing to another part of Bristol, Thomas Street. 'Well, certainly it is a long way from Thomas Street,' was the comment of Mrs Jenkins, who was probably not too upset at never having to see her uninvited and unstable guest again.

Two days later, Susan issued a summons for the maintenance arrears, which were paid on the following day.

On 17 August baby Sarah was a little unwell. Her gums were red and swollen and her breath smelt. Innocently, mother and grandmother stirred one of the powders into some soaked bread and sugar. The resulting mixture was light blue, but as the women had never seen a Steedman's powder before this did not arouse any suspicion. Neither of them thought to taste it. The mixture was fed to the child, who was most reluctant to take it, and as soon as it was eaten, she began to cry. Susan took her child out into the garden to soothe her, but she only cried harder and was heard to call out what sounded like 'Papa! Papa!' Soon the cries became screeches of agony, which brought Mrs Jenkins out into the garden to see what the matter was. Sarah's little body was rigid and arched, her face dark and her tiny fists clenched. At first Susan and her mother thought a pin had run into Sarah, but no pin could be found, and as the condition rapidly worsened the distraught women realised they needed a doctor. Susan ran to two local doctors, neither of whom was willing to come. She eventually found Dr Parsons, who lived a mile away. By the time he arrived the child was dead.

Two of the powders remained, and they were shown to the doctor. Cautiously, he touched one of them with his tongue, and noticed a metallic taste and a sickly sensation. He at once ordered that they be sent for analysis. The powders, the letter and the envelope they had arrived in were handed over to Constable Critchley. Critchley was well acquainted with Edwin Bailey and had correspond-ence from him which he was able to compare with the handwriting of the letter. He also noticed that the notepaper of the letter seemed identical to that used by Bailey. He made enquiries to see if there was a Jane Isabella Smith at Cotham, but there was no one there of that name, and the inhabitants of Hope Cottage had never heard of her. Critchley also established that in the previous year the Bristol Infirmary had had no patients called Elms or Nelmes.

Edwin Bailey came to hear of the death of little Sarah through an acquaintance of the Jenkins family, Thomas Parsons, who knew one of Bailey's employees. Shortly afterwards Parsons received from Bailey the sum of half a sovereign.

On 18 August Dr Parsons carried out the post-mortem on little Sarah and concluded that she had been poisoned by some metallic irritant, probably strychnine. He placed the stomach and intestines in a jar and this, together with the two remaining powders, were passed to the county analyst, Mr John Horsley. The first thing he noticed was that despite being enclosed in the correct papers for Steedman's powders, they were something very different. Steedman's powders, which contained half a grain of calomel (a gentle laxative) with sugar and cornflour, weighed only two and a quarter grains. These were twice the weight. He concluded that the Steedman's powders had been taken out of the wrappers and something else substituted. Analysis showed that the powders were in fact a product known as 'Vermin Killers'. Each one contained one-fifth of a grain of strychnine. One-sixteenth was enough to kill a small child. While his analysis of the intestines failed to discover any strychnine, the stomach contents showed traces of the same blue dye as was in the powders.

The inquest on little Sarah was formally opened at the Volunteer Inn on 18 August and adjourned to 5 September. At the second hearing Edwin Bailey was present and heard the evidence given by Constable Critchley about the notepaper. Bailey was bound over in the sum of £20 to appear at the adjourned hearing a week later but was unaccountably missing. Police Superintendent David Rawle said he had heard that Bailey had sailed for America, but Mr Clifton, his solicitor, said he had gone to London to see his wife. 'I never like to make *ex parte* observations,' said the coroner, Mr W. Gaisford, 'but I must say his absence is rather significant.' He issued a warrant for the arrest of Bailey on charges of contempt of court. Enquiries had revealed that Bailey employed a charwoman called Anne Barry, whose description fitted that of the lady who had visited the Jenkins family, and on 14 September she was arrested at her lodgings at St James's Back (now Silver Street), Bristol, where she had been living for the previous eight months. Anne's real name, it was reported, was Anne Salmond, and she lived with a common-law husband, Lewis Barry, a 36-year-old porter, who sometimes went under the name of Randolph, and had not long served three months in prison at Chichester. Soon after Anne was taken into custody he was arrested for a robbery in Cheltenham. Anne met her new situation with composure, and the newspapers were undecided as to whether she was of weak intellect and unaware of the danger she was in, or a callous woman with an iron will. She made the following statement: 'I was working for Mr Edwin Bailey, and I was often sent on errands to different places, and Mr Edwin Bailey sent me several times to the house where the illegitimate child of Mary [Susan] Jenkins was kept for the purpose if possible to get some tidings of who was the real father of the child, as he positively asserted it was not his, as he had nothing at all to do with her, and his object being to take it to a higher court; but as to anything about the poison, I know nothing about it.' It was suggested to her that she could very well save her life by giving evidence against Bailey, but this she firmly refused to do.

Bailey, advised by a friend that whether he was guilty or not the evidence was enough to put a rope around his neck, had decided to leave the country. Drawing a sum of money from the bank, he went to London, intending to sail for Spain. He had a final meeting with his wife, but she was anxious that the Clifton business, presumably her sole means of support, should not be given up, and asked him to go back there with her to show her what needed to be done. Bailey obligingly returned home and, undeterred by placards announcing the arrest of Anne Barry, donned his apron and busied himself in his shop, where he was seen and shortly afterwards arrested.

With the Horfield poisoning causing great excitement in Bristol, over in Arlingham, Deputy Chief Constable Griffin, who was not convinced that Edward Butt had drowned himself in the Severn, was doggedly making enquiries

The triple hanging. (Illustrated Police News, 1873)

throughout the county. Edward may have last been seen heading towards the river, but in Arlingham everyone knew that when the tide was low, as it had been at the time of Amelia's murder, it was possible to wade across. On Thursday 21 August, accompanied by two constables, Griffin rode to Arlingham. Leaving his horse and trap at the Red Lion Inn, he saw a similar vehicle with three or four people in it drive out of Mrs Butt's yard and pass him by in the direction of Gloucester. It had not gone far, however, when the horse's head was turned and the little party drove back to Mrs Butt's. This odd behaviour aroused Griffin's suspicions, and instead of making enquiries in other parts of the village as he had intended, he went directly to Church Farm. As he walked into the farmyard he saw the same trap hastily making off towards Gloucester again. Convinced that Mrs Butt had had some communication regarding her son, he entered the farmhouse and spoke to her. She admitted that she had received a letter which was currently in the possession of her sister, who was one of the occupants of the trap. The chase was on. Griffin rushed back to collect his horse and trap, and at once drove as fast as he could to overtake his quarry, which he did near

Frampton. They were obliged to stop, and Griffin descended from his trap and demanded the letter, which was given up to him. According to this communication Edward Butt was very much alive, and working for 1s (5p) a day plus food at a public house in Abergavenny (possibly the Farmer's Arms) under the name of Smith. The landlord, Mr Matthews, suspicious that his employee was using an assumed name, had looked in Edward's pocket book, learned his true name and address, and written a letter to his family. Griffin at once drove to Gloucester and telegraphed the superintendent of police at Abergavenny, sending him a description of Edward and asking for his arrest. By the time he arrived in Abergavenny Edward was already in custody. He was taken to Gloucester, where he made a full confession.

The trial of Edwin Bailey and Anne Barry opened at the Gloucester Assizes on 23 December 1873. Anne was described by the *Gloucester Journal* as 'a respectable-looking demure little woman neatly attired in mourning and with smooth glossy hair as black as her dress, her eyes seemed to glitter with suppressed excitement during the two days of the trial'. The two accused stood in the dock together, but rarely did they glance at each other. The prosecution brought the evidence of Mr Charles Chabot of London, a handwriting expert, who compared the letter and envelope with documents known to have been written by Edwin Bailey. Not only was the handwriting the same, there were also little peculiarities such as the contraction of August to Augst which were identical throughout the samples. The paper and the envelope were also the same as some found in Bailey's possession. No witness was brought by the defence to cast any doubt upon Chabot's evidence.

The jury deliberated for almost an hour. On the question of Bailey's guilt there was probably not a great deal of debate, as he was the only person with a motive to kill the child, but what of Anne Barry? Was she a part of the conspiracy or was she only an innocent dupe sent to run errands for her employer? The jury found Bailey guilty with a recommendation to mercy and Anne Barry guilty but with a strong recommendation to mercy. Bailey took the news calmly. 'I know nothing of it,' he said. 'Gentlemen, it is a conspiracy. I never wrote the letter. It is not the first time my handwriting has been forged.' The question of whether mercy was to be given was not a matter for that court, and the judge, as was his duty, donned the black cap and sentenced them both to hang.

The trial of Edward Butt was held on 24 December. He entered a plea of not guilty, the main plank of the defence being that it had all been an accident. It took the jury 15 minutes to find him guilty, and he was sentenced to death. He fainted and had to be carried from the court. A letter to the *Gloucester Journal* on 27 December expressed what must surely have been a widely held view, that the murder of Amelia Phipps, having taken place in a state of frenzied excitement, Edward Butt was far more deserving of mercy than the perpetrators of the murder of Sarah Jenkins, which had clearly been planned for many months. Public opinion was in fact very much against the hanging of all three culprits, Butt because of sympathy and Bailey and Barry because it was felt that the evidence against them was very slender. Petitions for a reprieve were drawn up and taken to Home Secretary Robert Lowe, and the jurors who had condemned Butt also wrote asking for mercy. The city waited. In prison Butt seemed calm and penitent. He was allowed a pint of beer a day, and the occasional pipe of tobacco. Bailey spent much of his time writing to his friends, asking them to campaign for his reprieve. One friend actually visited Susan Jenkins to ask her if she would help, but after that lady had provided a few home truths about Edwin Bailey he departed and took no further part in the campaign. Anne Barry remained calm and obstinately refused to admit her guilt.

The morning of 12 January was bleak and cold. A large and unusually quiet crowd gathered outside the prison from about 7 a.m. In the square, stone-walled execution yard busy preparations had been made. Prior executions had taken place on a platform 4–5ft high, obliging the prisoner to ascend a number of steps to his or her doom. For the triple execution a 'modern drop' would be used, abolishing the platform and using instead a pit about 5ft deep. Workmen had been busy digging the pit and had come across a part of the old city wall. The pit was covered with hinged doors, with a mechanism that would allow them to fall in at the pull of a rope. A black calico screen 4ft high had been placed across the apparatus, shielding spectators from the sight of the final death struggles. Shortly before 7.45 a.m. Mr Anderson the executioner came out 'skipping lightly . . . across the yard' and proceeded to attach the ropes to heavy chains which were fixed to the crossbar of the gallows by metal clamps. As he worked, the spectators, who consisted of prison officials, medical men, the high sheriff and his deputy and representatives of the press, assembled quietly. Anderson, a clean-shaven man with a keen expression, and, commented the *Gloucester Mercury*, 'nothing repulsive in his appearance', assured the assembly that the length of the ropes had been very carefully calculated. As the bell tolled 8 a.m. the three condemned prisoners, led by the chaplain, emerged into the yard, pale and flinching at the sight of the apparatus of death. The men wore grey suits, Barry a pale gown printed with sprays of lilac. All three were placed in position, Barry in the centre with Bailey to her left. All then knelt for prayers, during which they were entirely hidden by the screen. It was anticipated that they might be overcome by weakness, especially Barry, but when they all stood they were trembling but steady. The white caps and ropes were put in place, the legs of the prisoners were strapped and final prayers were said. As Anderson made the last adjustments Barry whispered to him that she had dreamed she would come to this end. Anderson pulled the rope, and as the drop fell there was a muffled gasp and a sob from the spectators. The execution was signalled to the outside world by the hoisting of a black flag. Shortly afterwards the chaplain revealed to the press that the previous evening both Bailey and Barry had confessed their guilt.

6

VIRTUE AND SIN

Oakridge Lynch, 1893

In the western Cotswolds the land is scored by deep valleys carved by ancient ice. The steep hillsides are thickly wooded and fast streams run far below. It is a landscape of great beauty and drama, dotted with picturesque villages and isolated farmhouses of local stone, connected by narrow, eccentrically winding lanes. For centuries the region's rivers have powered both silk and woollen mills, while the plateaux provide both arable and pastoral farmland. One such farm was known as Twissell's, from a family that once owned the land. The farm consisted of fertile meadows and orchards, the lower and upper portions divided by the village of Oakridge Lynch, with what had once been common land extending in the direction of Bisley.

In 1893 the farm was rented by 73-year-old James Wyndham, whose recent behaviour had both outraged the decency of his neighbours and alienated his children. His son Frederick had unfortunately inherited many of his father's character traits. Both were argumentative, impulsive and belligerent, and having once taken a course of action were, in the face of the most persuasive criticism, loudly and proudly unrepentant. Any interaction between the two was liable to be explosive.

The family name had once been Window. James was born in Nailsworth, and early in 1851 he and his wife Sarah Jemima were living in the village of Newmarket, where he worked as a bacon curer's labourer. There were already five children of the family: two sons, including 3-year-old Frederick, and three daughters. A fourth daughter, Susan Smith Window, was born later that year, and another son and two more daughters were to follow. Family life was sometimes tempestuous, as James could be violent and quarrelsome. Once, when Frederick was about 10 or 12 years of age, his father had taken the boy up to the attic and left him standing up, his thumbs tied to a beam, for a day and a night. The family was forbidden to go to him during this time, but Sarah had defied her husband and crept upstairs to give Frederick some food. After another childhood misdemeanour, Frederick had been obliged to jump in the millpond to escape his father's wrath, but James had pursued him and threw a stone which injured the back of his son's head.

Chalford, near Oakridge, in the early twentieth century. (Author's collection)

James turned to farming, an occupation in which his growing family assisted. In 1871 he was working 139 acres at Tunley and employing one man. The family had undergone a surname change, recorded in the census of that year as Windham, though in later years it was spelt Wyndham. In 1881 James was working 169 acres of land at Twissell's Farm, Oakridge Lynch, employing three men, a woman and a boy, and living in Frampton Place farmhouse.

Frederick married Ellen Hill in 1871; the couple settled in Stroud and raised five children. Of all the family his surname is most frequently spelt Windham in official records. Over the years Frederick's relationship with his father had mellowed, and he was not lacking in filial duty, for on more than one occasion he had driven his father home when the old man was helplessly drunk, lifted him out of the trap, settled him in his armchair and walked the 5 miles back home to Stroud. In 1881 he was working a milk round, but that enterprise failed and he was unemployed for a while. In 1891 the family was living in Summer Street and Frederick was a butcher, but at the beginning of 1893 he found employment with 26-year-old farmer and coal merchant William David Farrar, as bailiff of Abbey Farm.

In 1889 Sarah Jemima died. It is not unknown for a widower approaching 70 to look for a new wife, but what distinguished James Wyndham from other men of his age was his obsession with finding a spirited sexual partner and the determined manner in which he worked his way through the more obliging women of the district.

St Bartholomew's Church, Oakridge Lynch. (Author's collection)

He finally settled on a lady by the name of Virtue Mills. Born Virtue Frances Hunt in 1848 she was the daughter of a plasterer, Jeremiah Hunt of Bisley. In 1873 she married William Mills, a London-born horsebreaker living in Stroud. By 1881, however, the couple had parted, and Virtue, working as a stickmaker, had gone back to live with her mother. When James announced that he would be bringing Virtue Mills into the house, the unmarried daughters who still lived with their father, and who must have known something about Mrs Mills which was not revealed publicly, all stated that they would not live with such a woman. Susan and Frederick had remonstrated with their father, but he said that he 'had tried a dozen whores and he liked this one the best. He had the biggest whore he could find.' Soon afterwards the remaining family departed, leaving James on the farm with only Virtue Mills for company. In the 1891 census she is described as a 'housekeeper', though there was no doubt as to her actual role. Many local people nonetheless believed that the couple were man and wife, so it later came as something of a surprise to the village to find that not only were they not married, but Virtue had a husband still living.

It was Frederick who was the most violently opposed to his father's liaison with Mrs Mills, and he often threatened to shoot her. He told Enoch Horsham, an innkeeper, that his father had acted very cruelly to him and the family, turning his daughters out of the house and taking in a woman as housekeeper whom he called a prostitute. He said that if James did not turn her out of the house he would blow his father's brains out. If these threats were frequent it was not surprising that no one took them seriously.

Despite this anger and resentment Frederick remained on speaking terms with James, who had given him permission to come and shoot game on his farm. A few weeks before their final, violent confrontation James had given Frederick a coat and waistcoat.

Susan and her father had an additional dispute. James had some money belonging to her and refused to hand it over, so she had engaged a solicitor to write to him asking for its return. In September 1893 Susan was in Holloway Road, Oakridge, with two friends, Sarah Jane Gardiner and Emily Davis, when they encountered James, who swore at his daughter. The women continued to walk, and had gone a little way when they heard the sound of someone driving a horse and cart furiously fast behind them. They moved into single file close by the wall to allow the driver to pass, but Miss Gardiner, who was nearest, had to act fast so as not to be run over, since the driver, whom she recognised as James Wyndham, deliberately drove straight at her. 'Quick, Sue, jump over the wall!' she exclaimed, making her own escape, and Susan quickly flung herself into the adjoining field. It was a close call. James, unable and apparently unwilling either to stop or turn the cart, would undoubtedly have run her over if she had not made that desperate leap.

Susan, knowing that Frederick was very excitable, wisely did not mention the incident to him. James, however, went to Stroud and told Frederick's wife that he had tried to kill his daughter and would have done so, except she had kept in the field where he could not get at her. It is not surprising that Ellen repeated the story to her husband. Susan decided to get a solicitor to write to her father, and this was done. On 13 October the Stow-on-the-Wold firm of Francis and Son wrote to Susan:

Dear Madam

I am sorry to hear of your father's cruel and alarming conduct towards you and your friends. As suggested we have written to him to complain of his behaviour and telling him that you will be compelled to take legal proceedings on any repetition of the offence, and that the fact of his being your father alone prevents you from taking that course on the present occasion.

We hope this may keep him in check, but you will certainly be wise in avoiding him where possible.

On Wednesday 18 October Frederick and William Farrar agreed to go shooting game at Twissell's Farm on the following day. They had done so a few weeks previously, on which occasion Farrar and his 15-year-old brother Harold had gone into the farmhouse for some refreshments, but Frederick had refused to go in, presumably because he didn't want to confront Virtue Mills, so his father had sent refreshments out to him. Farrar agreed to the expedition, mainly because he wanted the opportunity to drive a pony that had only recently been placed in harness. He therefore told Frederick to get the pony and trap and meet him on Stroud Hill at 11 a.m. The two men, accompanied by Harold Farrar, drove up to Oakridge. On the way they stopped briefly at Bisley, as Frederick wanted to see Susan, who was lodging at the New Inn, run by a Mr and Mrs Skinner. Farrar was in the passage as they talked, but he was able to overhear the conversation. After asking how she was, Frederick said, 'The old man tried to drive over you, didn't he?' Susan said he had, but that she had cautioned him and didn't think he would do it again, and she showed him the solicitor's letter. Frederick said his father would never have done it if he, Frederick, had been there.

Farrar ordered a pint of cider at the inn, of which Frederick consumed half, while his companion had lemonade. Frederick then borrowed a gun from Mr Skinner, a double-barrelled breech-loader, and put it in the trap. He had forgotten to bring Farrar's gun, so Harold had to be sent back for it. In the end they did not arrive at Twissell's Farm until 1 p.m. Farrar knew Frederick to be of an excitable

The Butcher's Arms Inn, Oakridge Lynch. (By kind permission of the landlord)

nature, but on this occasion saw that his companion was in an especially agitated state. They went into the nearby Butcher's Arms Inn, where Frederick drank a pint of cider; they then took their guns and went out to the farm. There they spotted Farrar's father on the canal side and went over to talk to him. All the men then went into The Oak beer house in Frampton parish, where Frederick had another glass of cider. Finally they went back to the cover to shoot game. Here 21-year-old Gilbert Rawle, a grocer's assistant of Chalford Hill, appeared with a gun and two dogs. Frederick and Harold approached him, and Frederick demanded to know what business he had there. Rawle said that he had permission from James to shoot on the land, but Frederick was having none of it. He took away a rabbit the man had shot and said that if he caught him there again he would throw him in the brook. The party then returned to the Butcher's Arms for something to eat. Farrar drank lemonade, but Frederick had another pint of cider, enlivened by the addition of a tot of rum. When they emerged at 3.30 p.m. Rawle had gone. Farrar and Frederick walked on, sending Harold up ahead with the pony and trap.

It was nearly 4 p.m. when they saw James at work on the far side of the field by Baker's Barn, lifting potatoes. With him were farm workers Elizabeth Halliday and Arthur Stevens, an army reserve man. Farrar decided to go and speak to him. He asked Frederick if he was going to speak to his father, but Frederick said, 'No; let us go on.' Farrar and James chatted briefly, and James said he had no objections to their being there. Frederick then approached, and there was some discussion about the coat and waistcoat he was wearing – the same ones his father had given him. Inevitably the conversation soon deteriorated into a quarrel about Mrs Mills, Frederick saying it was a disgrace to the family, his father having such a woman living with him. He also demanded to know what his father meant by attempting to drive over Susan, to which the old man replied that he would do just as he pleased. He rebuked his son for talking about family matters in front of his employees. James, drawing the obvious conclusion from the aroma of cider that must have been on his son's breath, said, 'I am sorry to see you here like this; you are drunk.' Frederick, who was by now trembling with anger, retorted that whatever was the matter with him, it was due to the 'whore' with whom his father lived. The three men were walking to the next field; they went through the gate into ploughed ground, which lay some 400 yards from the main Bisley to Oakridge road, father and son wrangling as they went, James's dog trotting by his side. Frederick asked his father whether he had got the lawyer's letter, but James made no reply. Frederick then tasked him about Rawle's shooting there. James protested that Rawle had his permission and was a steady man. Frederick told his father he had met Rawle, taken away the rabbit and threatened to throw him in the brook if he caught him again. 'Then you have very much upset me,' said his father, 'and I shan't give you permission to come here again.'

On the footpath outside the field Mrs Georgina Stephens of Water Lane was on her way home. She saw Frederick arguing with his father and wildly waving his gun, so she stopped to peer over the wall. The two men were about 10 yards

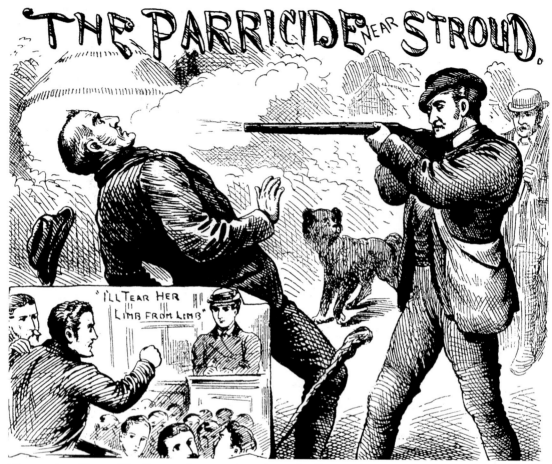

The murder of James Wyndham and a scene from the trial. (*Illustrated Police News*, 4 November 1893)

apart, squaring up to each other as if they were going to fight. As they neared each other Farrar, now very much alarmed, got in between them. He caught hold of Frederick and tried to remonstrate with him. He urged there should be no fighting, as his father could give leave to anyone he liked to go shooting, adding that he himself would not go there again.

Frederick, taking no notice at all of Farrar, called out that he would shoot the 'whore', then turned and walked back towards where the trap was waiting, muttering and swearing. Farrar followed, hopeful that the incident was over, but Frederick could not let it go. He turned around to look at his father, who was walking back to his potato field. Farrar could see that Frederick was in a tearing rage and tried to get him to go into the trap. This was the moment when James should have continued walking, but he did not – he turned and faced his angry son, and started towards him. Again Farrar tried to get Frederick to leave, but the two warring men came closer still, and they were only a few yards apart when Frederick said 'I will shoot you.' Then he put his gun to his shoulder and fired twice. The first charge tore across his father's shoulder and into the neck, leaving a wound some 1½ inches across. James staggered but didn't fall, and Frederick, without changing posture, fired again. The charge entered the chest, shattering the base of the heart. James dropped to the ground. Farrar, just yards away, could only watch in horror.

'I've shot my father under the earhole!' Frederick exclaimed, flinging up his arms and waving the gun around his head. Farrar's first thought was to get back to Bisley and report what had happened to the police. He did not approach James, whom he was sure was dead, and later admitted he was also afraid of the dog which was guarding its master's body. Instead, he accompanied Frederick back to the trap, which was waiting in another field. On the way they saw Mrs Stephens looking over the wall. Farrar asked her if she had seen what had happened. She replied that she had and wished now she had not come that way. As they walked, Frederick asked Farrar for two more cartridges so he could blow his own brains out. Farrar refused to give him any. Frederick actually had two undischarged cartridges in his pocket, a fact which he had forgotten. As they approached the trap Farrar called out to Harold, 'He has shot his father!'

'No!' said Harold, but Frederick confirmed it was true. He put the gun in the trap and started to walk away, saying that he would go and tell his sister what he had done and then give himself up, but Farrar persuaded him to get into the trap and they drove away.

In the potato field farm worker Arthur Stevens had heard the first shot and an exclamation, and jumping up on the shaft of his cart saw James's hat flying off. Next moment there was another report, and he saw James fall. 'Good God! They have been and shot Mr Wyndham,' he exclaimed. Stevens ran to the field, where he saw Frederick and Farrar walking away from his stricken master. James lay on his right side, legs doubled up and hands clenched, bleeding profusely. There were marks of blood and pieces of bone on the ground for 4 yards from where the body lay. Stevens, showing remarkable presence of mind and efficiency, at once took charge of the situation. He checked James's pulse and spoke to him. Noting that his master was dead, he sent for the doctor and the police. He spoke to Mrs Stephens, established that she had seen what had happened, and took her name and address before allowing her to leave. He then remained with the body, making his own careful observation of the scene until help came.

Meanwhile, Frederick and the Farrars drove back to Bisley. William Farrar drove, until he found he couldn't manage the pony down the hill, whereupon he gave the reins to Frederick. As they drove along, Frederick told Farrar to see that his dog was given to his sister Emily and, anticipating that he would very soon be in the county gaol, asked whether Farrar would come and visit him. At last they reached the New Inn, where Frederick went in to see Susan. 'I have done it,' he announced. 'I have shot my father. I will die for you. He'll drive over you no more.' This was overheard by Mrs Skinner, whose cries of alarm attracted a crowd. Leaving his gun behind at the inn, Frederick walked up the road to the police station, pausing only to turn to the crowd and cry, 'I have shot my father',

Probable site of the murder of James Wyndham, Oakridge Lynch. (Author's collection)

throwing his arms wildly above his head. He then continued to walk up to the police station.

PC Henry Hoskins was on duty in Bisley police station with PC Gwinnell when there was a tremendous rap on the door, and Frederick walked in. 'I want one of you to come with me,' he announced. 'I have been and shot my father, and if he is not dead, I hope he is.' Hoskins advised Frederick to be careful what he said, but Frederick simply repeated his statement. Hoskins searched Frederick and found two cartridges in his jacket pocket. 'I shall put you in the cell,' he said.

'You won't do that unless you are a better man than me,' retorted Frederick. Hoskins obviously was, since he was able, with a certain amount of force, to get Frederick into a cell. Thereafter the prisoner's manner was calm and composed. Hoskins left the station only to bump into Farrar, who confirmed what Frederick had said and handed in the gun. With the gun safely stowed in the station, Hoskins asked Farrar to drive him to the scene, but Farrar was most unwilling to return, protesting that the pony was too young, and a passer-by offered to transport him.

There was some difficulty in approaching the body, as the dog growled at the approach of strangers, and had to be driven away with stones. The body was taken to the Butcher's Arms Inn, where it was washed and laid out. Dr Gordon arrived and, from what the coroner later described as 'an excess of zeal', removed five shots from the neck. Later he conducted a full post-mortem.

Superintendent Harrison and Sergeant Browning of Stroud police station went to Bisley to conduct Frederick to Stroud. They had Frederick taken to the guard room for questioning. His first words to them were, 'I only done my duty.' Harrison advised him that he was charged with the wilful murder of his father and gave him the usual caution to be careful what he said. Frederick made a statement, which was taken down in writing.

'I solemnly declare that I shot him. Put two barrels into him. I hope he is dead. He is dead, I hope; and I can die happy in a minute.' Frederick then signed the statement.

That evening large crowds of people waited at the junction of the roads at the bottom of the High Street in excited expectation of seeing Frederick brought into Stroud. The whole town was buzzing with the news, although the facts of the case were somewhat unclear. At 10.30 p.m. a commotion announced the approach of the prisoner. Frederick rode in a close fly, escorted by Sergeant Browning and PC Hoskins, with Superintendent Harrison following in his trap.

Frederick was typically unrepentant. 'If I had my liberty now,' he told the policemen, 'and knew the old bugger was not dead, I'd go back and put another charge in him.'

High Street, Stroud, 1910. (Author's collection)

As they processed along the High Street, some people followed behind them while others ran on down towards the police station. There Frederick was removed from the fly. Just before he entered the station he turned to the crowds and said, 'Good night, all; I've done my duty.' 'Good night, Fred,' said a few sympathetic voices, but most were silent, or commented among themselves as to the coolness of his behaviour.

He was equally cool at the hearing before the magistrates at 2.30 p.m. the following day. The main controversy was how to spell his surname, and the prisoner decided to own to the name of Fred Window. He was remanded for a week. While in Stroud he was visited by Enoch Horsham, who asked him what had possessed him to do such a thing. 'I made up my mind to do it before I left in the morning,' he revealed, 'and that's why I borrowed Skinner's gun.'

The inquest on James Wyndham took place at the Butcher's Arms Inn, Oakridge, on 21 October, commencing at 11 a.m. The jury having been sworn, they were taken to view the body, which lay in an adjoining house. Some surprise was expressed that Farrar had not approached James after the shooting or attempted to give any help. Arthur Stevens was praised for having given his evidence in a very straightforward way. It was felt that he had made up for what the coroner was beginning to feel was the neglect of others.

Frederick was taken to Gloucester Gaol by train, astonishing his escorts by laughing and joking with them, and commenting to the newsboys that their papers would sell well that night.

On the Sunday following the murder the district's clergymen saw solemn lessons for their flock in the tragic events. The Revd Ormerod of Stroud parish church, who had once been vicar of Oakridge and who knew the family, took as his text 'Fathers provoke not your children to wrath and children obey your parents in all things.' At Holy Trinity in Stroud, the church where Frederick and his family worshipped, the Revd Hawkins asked the congregation to pray for Frederick's wife and children.

James Wyndham's funeral took place on Tuesday 24 October. A large crowd had gathered outside the gate of the farm, whence the cortège left at about 3 p.m. The body was taken in a glass-sided hearse. Many of James's workmen attended as mourners, as did his son Henry and some nephews. One person not present was Mrs Virtue Mills. She had wanted to attend but in view of the bad relations between herself and the deceased's family she had been persuaded not to. She had instead gone to stay with a sister at Far Oakridge.

The procession travelled half a mile to the church, where it was met by the vicar, the Revd Doherty. It is often said that one should never speak ill of the dead, and at a funeral it is traditional to remember the best of a person's life. The funeral address of the Revd Doherty, however, was both startling and original. He told the mourners that he and the farmer had been friends. He knew him to be just and fair in financial matters and always ready to help his neighbours, but unhappily their cordial relations had come to an end when James had entered on a course of life of which the vicar could not approve. He had spoken to the old man about the consequences of trampling upon God's holy laws and urged him to turn away from this path. But his words had been of no avail, and from that moment James had taken no notice of him. Doherty warned the astounded congregation against giving way to sins of lust and passion, for they could never know where it would lead. The path of sin was the path of danger, and they should look to God's grace to give them the power to control their passions. From the back of the church a voice rang out loudly that the vicar ought to apologise for his words, but Doherty took no notice. The address done, the mourners proceeded to the grave, where it was suddenly discovered that the opening was not large enough to take the coffin. Henry almost fainted from distress, and the ceremony was held up while the grave was enlarged.

On 26 October Frederick was brought before the magistrates at Stroud police station. On the way he told his escorts that his actions were purely a matter of duty, and his only regret was not having shot Mrs Mills, too. The court was crowded with people, including many children, who kept up a constant hum of conversation as they stared at the dishevelled and unshaven Frederick.

When Susan, looking strained and haggard, gave her evidence, Frederick leaned forward over the rail with tears in his eyes, but when Virtue Mills was called he at once asked to be allowed to leave the court. This not being permitted, he asked for a revolver. As Virtue entered the witness box he began to hiss and threaten her, saying, 'I'd like to get hold of her.' He watched, pale and restless, as she gave evidence, continually muttering under his breath and hissing. He was repeatedly asked by the police and magistrates to keep quiet but took no notice. Virtue was dressed all in black with a large hat with which she managed to hide most of her face. She said Frederick had come to the door when she was in the house but always refused to come in. She had heard him quarrelling with his father and had also heard him threaten to kill him. On one occasion the two men had been at the iron gates of the house, quarrelling for nearly half an hour, and when James came in he had a mouth full of blood. At this statement Frederick turned round and faced the wall, weeping and trembling. Only gradually did he become calmer, and turned back to face the court. When Virtue said she had left her husband because he would not work to get an honest living, Frederick shouted out that he had left her because she was bad, and continued to hurl abuse and threats. As she stepped down he cried, 'Let me get at her for two minutes and I'll tear her limb from limb. I could cut her to pieces! Nothing is too bad for her. She'd better jump in the canal and drown herself!'

Frederick was committed for trial at the Gloucester Assizes, which commenced on Tuesday 28 November 1893 before Mr Justice Cave, the court being packed with spectators. Counsel for the defence Mr Gwynne James had a hard task, and indeed the only extenuating circumstance he could suggest was that his client was insane. Frederick had been determined to plead guilty, and it was only with great difficulty that his counsel persuaded him to enter a not guilty plea. Frederick arrived in the dock with a firm step. He was well aware of how it would end for him. When Susan described how Frederick had said 'I will die for you', the

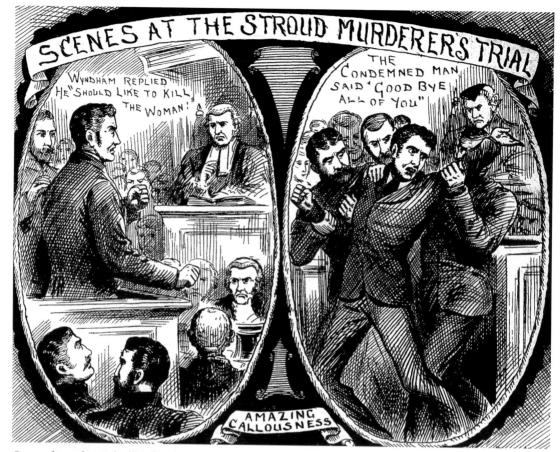

Scenes from the trial of Frederick Wyndham. (Illustrated Police News, 4 November 1893)

prisoner cried out in a loud voice, 'And so I will.'

Susan gave evidence about how her father had turned his children out of the house. Mr James was about to question her on the previous relations between Frederick and his father when His Lordship interposed, saying he failed to see how it could affect the case. Mr James replied that it would show what his line of defence was. 'It does not justify a man shooting his father,' said Cave. 'It is to show the treatment the prisoner was subjected to,' said counsel.

'Absolutely nothing to do with the case,' said Cave. 'He has paid a terrible penalty, and it does not look well to bring his children here to blacken his character.'

'Surely the bringing up of this man may have had something to do with his mental condition,' pleaded Mr James. 'I should think nothing at all,' said his Lordship. 'It was years ago.'

In his address to the jury, counsel for the defence maintained that Frederick had been insane when he killed his father, and that he had not known that what he was doing was wrong. It was open to them to bring in a verdict of guilty but insane, whereupon his client would spend the rest of his life in an asylum. At this, Frederick cried out, 'No! No!'

The defence called no witnesses, and it only remained for Mr Justice Cave to sum up. He pointed out that the very act of going to the police and giving himself up suggested that Frederick was well aware that he had done something for which he was liable to be arrested. No doctor, no single piece of evidence had come before the court to show that the prisoner was insane, and there was abundant evidence that he knew what he was doing. The jury, without retiring, consulted for less than two minutes before bringing a verdict of guilty.

Frederick stepped up to the front of the dock to hear his sentence. Asked if he had anything to say, he replied, 'I should like to kill the woman.' As the judge donned the black cap Frederick pointed to Virtue Mills, who had come to watch the trial, and cried out, 'She is the cause of all of it.' The judge said he hoped that the prisoner would spend his remaining time in repentance, but Frederick shouted out, 'I will not repent for killing him.'

Frederick was sentenced to death by hanging. He thanked the judge and, before being removed from the dock, turned and said to everyone, 'Goodbye all of you.'

As the case ended Virtue Mills was recognised and mobbed on leaving the Shire Hall. She had intended to visit some friends on the outskirts of Gloucester, but the surging crowd, which was composed mainly of women, hustled her about so much that she was obliged on reaching Barton Crossing to seek refuge in the signal box. The police and a passing clergyman took pity on her, dispersed the

The assize judges arriving for a Sunday service at Gloucester Cathedral, c. 1910. (Sutton Collection)

angry mob and escorted her to the railway station, from where she was able to make her escape.

Frederick awaited execution with no change in his defiant and unrepentant manner. He seemed indifferent to his fate, and his family and friends decided not to petition the Home Office for a reprieve. When told by the under-sheriff that his execution had been set for 21 December he asked if it couldn't be done earlier, as three weeks was a long time to wait.

The condemned cell was on the top floor of the oldest part of the prison, isolated from the other buildings, the windowless space separated from the guard room by a doorway with an iron grating. A narrow winding staircase led down to the execution yard which was open to the sky, and from which, behind some iron palings, could be seen the grassy burial ground. Before the execution a piece of board was placed against the palings so that the condemned man would not be able to see his own grave.

There was universal sympathy for Frederick's family, and a Mrs Pegler of Bisley Old Road started a subscription for the household. Frederick himself was generally held to have deserved his fate. The *Gloucester Journal* concluded that 'the culprit's heart is of hardness and blackness which are only to be associated with an intelligence of the most low and depraved type', while the *Gloucester Chronicle* said that any spark of sympathy for him had been extinguished by his

The old Gloucester Penitentiary (from an eighteenth-century print).

Death certificate of Frederick Wyndham. (By permission of HMSO)

manner in the dock, and that he must be 'a man of a most callous nature'. Susan later wrote to the *Stroud News* and stated, 'My brother has told me he had no intention of killing my father till the moment he did it. My brother's mind has been weak from a boy, as he tried to take his own life when he was the age of seventeen, and within the last three years he has also several times attempted to do so.' The editor commented that, had the facts been known earlier, 'many would view the terrible action of the condemned man in quite a different light'.

At the appointed hour Frederick was brought into the yard bareheaded and in his shirtsleeves. On being handed over to the executioners, Mr Billington and his assistant, he cordially shook hands with them and wished them good morning before submitting quietly to being pinioned. Looking at the press representatives he said, 'I wish you all goodbye. I should like to have killed that whore before I died.' As the cap was being put on he cried out, 'Ready.' The noose was tightened, the lever was pulled, and he plunged 6 feet to die instantly.

James Wyndham's will, drawn up while his wife was still alive, bequeathed property to the value of £339 15s 6d (£339.78) entirely to her, and in the event of her predeceasing him all was placed in trust to be divided equally between his children. There was no mention of Virtue Mills.

7
THE MAD CYCLIST

Horsley and Saddlewood, 1902

The ancient parish of Horsley, near Stroud, with its woods, farmlands and winding lanes, is a peaceful and picturesque spot. A church was recorded there as early as 1105, and the village developed around a nearby crossroads. Its heyday was the 1830s, when farming and weaving supported a population of nearly 3,700, but with the decline of the cloth industry many families departed. By the end of the nineteenth century there were just over 1,000 inhabitants.

Horsley village, early twentieth century. (Contemporary postcard)

South of the church, on the summit of a hill, stands a handsome country house, large and square, with an imposing presence and a long history. There was once a priory there, but it was closed in 1380 and fell into ruins, although its old chapel and gateway remained on the site for another 400 years. The land was used for the construction of a prison, which opened in 1791, and in addition to the cells there was a court, a chapel, two dwellings and a lodge. The prison closed in 1878 and most of the buildings were demolished, but a three-storey block was converted for use as a residence. In view of the history of the site it was called the Priory.

There are other fine buildings in the area. Barton End House, originally a seventeenth-century farmhouse, has later extensions and was once the home of the poet Sydney Dobell. In 1901 it had for many years been occupied by Laurence Williams, JP, a retired army major, who was a prominent and respected figure in the community. He and his wife Eliza brought up a family of five daughters and two sons. Marshall Bruce Williams, their eldest boy, was born in 1863 and William Wright Williams in 1865. The sons were educated at boarding school. The 1881 census finds 18-year-old Marshall at Cheltenham College, while 15-year-old William was at Felstead Grammar School, Essex. It is not known what profession their father had hoped they would follow, but in 1901 Marshall was without an occupation, and William, who had a reputation for eccentricity and was not on good terms with his father, had gone to Canada (some newspapers said California) where, according to his family, he was a 'rancher'. In the summer of 1901 William returned home. He was no nearer settling on a steady profession and spent most of his time amusing himself, staying either with his family at Barton End House or in London hotels.

Barton End House and the Priory being the two most substantial properties in the area, it was natural that their occupants should strike up an acquaintance, and William Williams became close friends with the Priory's young owner, John Dudley Scott, another young man with time on his hands. John Scott had been born in Hove in October 1874. His father, Robert Herries Dudley Scott, was a colliery proprietor who, dying when John was only 5 years of age, provided a legacy which ensured that, on reaching adulthood, his son would be a man of independent means. John, adopting the middle name Dudley, was married in 1898 to Evelyn Henrietta Knocker, whose father was town clerk of Dover. They bought the Priory, and two children were born: a son, Herries Knocker Scott, in 1899 and a daughter, Aurora, in 1901.

Scott was of studious habits and his main hobby was book-collecting. Contemporary opinions recorded in the newspapers differed as to whether Scott was medium height and slightly built or tall and athletic, but it was generally agreed that he was smaller and fairer than the tall, sombre, powerfully built William Williams. The two men were very different in temperament, Scott being quiet, affable and friendly, Williams erratic and tempestuous, but a mutual love of books brought them together as friends and they began to spend a great deal of time together.

Horsley, c. *1909.* (Contemporary postcard)

The men's main recreation was cycling. 'In years to come,' commented the *Stroud Journal*, 'the historian will probably reckon cycling among the great expanding and formative influences of the latter part of the nineteenth century and the opening years of the twentieth century. Cycles have had a large share in taking the people out of themselves and their narrow surroundings and familiarizing them with a great world quite out of their reach but for the swift, silent and obedient steel steed.' The frequent references to cycling in the local press show that in Stroud and the nearby villages it was enormously popular, both as a means of getting about and as a pastime, the hard chalky roads providing an ideal surface. William's only other recreation was playing billiards at the George Hotel, Stroud, where he was thought to be rather odd, as he would play for hours on end without speaking a word to anyone.

In May 1902 the Williams family decided to quit Barton End House, and the property was put up for sale in June. William found this prospect highly disturbing, and as the day of the sale approached he gave vent to dark utterances about 'doing for' someone, utterances that were so alarming that the police kept him under surveillance. Scott offered to let his unhappy friend stay at the Priory, and after the Williams family left Horsley to reside in Surrey, William spent most of his time with the Scotts, apart from the occasional trip to London. There was another factor that might have affected his mood. The Scotts had decided to move out of the Priory. They had found a tenant for it and were hoping to sell the property. Quite when this was to happen or where they were intending to go was not revealed in the press.

It is not unusual for a young wife to take a dislike to one of her husband's closest friends, and as it turned out Mrs Scott was to show herself to have better judgement of character than her husband. 'Mrs Scott', her father later stated, 'was only glad to see Williams on account of her husband, who required company.' For some months before the tragedy that was to occur William's behaviour was such that the people he came in contact with had reason to doubt his sanity, an opinion which the mild, easy-going Scott seemed not to share. In August 1902 a tradesman of Stroud had to tell William to keep out of his shop in future because of the brutal way in which he spoke to the lady of the establishment. William would often enter the shop and ask for an item, but before it could even be brought to him he would curse and stamp out again. People were naturally wary of him and his only close associates were his brother Marshall and John Scott.

On Thursday 14 August William Williams was at the Priory. Mrs Scott had gone to Sevenoaks with the children to stay with her brother, so the only other occupants of the house were John Scott and the servants. It was the habit of the two men to go out for a cycle ride after dinner, and that evening, having dined at 7.30 p.m., they took their bicycles and set off at 9 p.m. It was a moonlit night, with a touch of mist. The roads in the area were ill-frequented, and it was possible to travel for many miles seeing neither people nor habitations, the only sound being the distant tinkle of a sheep bell. They probably cycled to Wotton

The Priory, Horsley, early twentieth century. (Contemporary postcard)

Gateway to Saddlewood Farm. (Author's collection)

under Edge before turning to go back via the main Bath to Gloucester road. One or two people sighted them along the way, but only one witness thought that they had been having 'high words'. Shortly after 10 p.m. John Bryan Till, a brewery clerk, was driving in a pony and trap with a friend to Nailsworth. Just as they reached the turning to Tresham, about 200 yards from the entrance gate to the drive that led to Saddlewood Farm, they passed two men pushing their bicycles up the incline, and Till recognised one of them as William Williams. It was a lonely spot, the nearest dwelling being the farmhouse half a mile east, which was not visible from the road, while a few of the houses of Hawkesbury Upton could be seen some 3 miles away. At about 11.30 p.m. PC Charles Gabb, who had often seen the two men ride out at 9 p.m. and return late, saw William Williams going towards the Priory pushing his bicycle, which had no light. He waited a few moments, expecting to see Scott following, but Williams was alone.

Martha Wilkins, a 30-year-old servant at the Priory, was quite used to the men returning late from such excursions, and sometimes not until the following day. Where they went and what they did she was not in a position to enquire. That Thursday she waited up for them until 11.15 p.m., and then went to bed. At 11.30 p.m. she heard someone come in and then go into the library, but whoever it was went out again very shortly afterwards.

At half past midnight, about a mile from Stroud, PC H.B. Medhurst saw a man riding a bicycle without a light and stopped him. The man explained that he had no acetylene and it was very important that he should be in Stroud that night. He added that he was well known in the area, being the son of Major Williams. Constable Medhurst took the rider's name – William Williams – in order to summons him later on a charge of riding without a light. William looked agitated and shaky, and the constable thought he might have been going to see someone who was ill, so he let him ride on. William arrived at Stroud railway station just before 1 a.m., where he left the bicycle in the charge of porter Henry Beard before catching the express to London. It reached Paddington shortly after 3 a.m., and he at once hired a hansom cab.

On the night of 14 to 15 August Marshall Bruce Williams was staying at the Golden Cross Hotel, Charing Cross, London. That morning he had telegraphed John Scott at the Priory to see if his brother was there and received a reply saying that he was. He expected William to depart for the Continent the following day and wanted to see him before he left, but he was not expecting him to turn up in the middle of the night. At 3.30 a.m. Marshall was asleep in bed when there was a knock at his door. Still groggy with sleep he got out of bed and unlocked the door. William entered in a state of nervous agitation and said that he had killed John Scott. Marshall, having just been awoken, could be excused for not taking the matter entirely seriously, especially as he knew his brother was not always to be relied upon to tell the truth. 'It was a very silly thing to do,' he said. 'What did you do it for?' The brothers talked for about half an hour. William, who spent most of the time restlessly pacing about the room, seemed depressed and unwilling to give much detail of events, but commented that what he had done was the best thing for Mrs Scott, and that he was going to give himself up to the police. Marshall told William to go to Batt's Hotel and get some sleep, and they would talk about it in the morning. While he did not necessarily accept that William had killed Scott, he was beginning to believe that Scott had at least been wounded, and certainly that something serious had happened. Despite this he contacted no one. William departed and at 4.45 a.m. he checked into Batt's Hotel, 41 Dover Street. He had stayed there before, so the fact that he was without luggage did not excite suspicion; neither did Charles Davis, the night porter, notice anything unusual in his manner, although the new guest seemed irritable and impatient.

At the Priory Emily Hammond the parlour maid was up early on the Friday morning. Going into Mr Williams's bedroom she found that the guest had not slept there, but the coat, waistcoat and shirt he had been wearing the previous night were lying on the floor. She picked them up and found that the shirt was still damp with sweat, and there were dirt and grass stains on the coat. Scott had not returned home at all, but since this was not unusual Emily continued about her duties unperturbed.

At 8 a.m. Thomas Richings, a shepherd employed by William Iles of Saddlewood Farm, was walking along the driveway towards the road when he found a bicycle lying in a quarry in a field about 130 yards from the gate. Continuing on his way he reached the outer gate, where he saw some oily rags, an oil can and a spanner lying in the roadway. Assuming that a cyclist had met with an accident there, he placed the items by the low wall that skirted a small coppice near the gate. Chancing to peer over the wall he saw, partially hidden by undergrowth, the body of a man lying face down. He could see at once that there had been foul play. Someone had made a deliberate effort to conceal the corpse by pushing it under some bushes and covering the head and shoulders with torn-up clumps of long grass. Richings at once ran to the farmhouse to tell Iles, who told him to notify Didmarton police station, some 2 miles away. Dr Forty of Wotton-under-Edge was summoned to the scene and, on examining the body, saw blood and brains oozing from a bullet hole behind the left ear. There could be no doubt that it was a case of murder. Blood on the roadway showed where the shooting had occurred – right in front of the gate – and the victim must have been riding his bicycle at the time, since there were marks showing where the bicycle had fallen, its pedal cutting into the road. Long smears of blood showed that the killer had then dragged the body along the ground, through the gate, and finally lifted it over the wall. The long grass that grew thickly in the area had been pulled up and strewn over the body. The victim's bicycle had then been wheeled down the driveway and thrown into the quarry. Nearby lay the dead man's cap. The area of deep undergrowth in the coppice rarely came under any scrutiny, and if it had not been for Richings's casual glance over the wall the body could well have lain there for much longer before being discovered. None of the deceased's belongings had been touched – he still wore a gold ring and a gold watch, and there was money in his pocket. Cards found in his letter case revealed his identity. He was John Dudley Scott.

The first theory was that Scott had been killed by strangers, and constables were at once dispatched to ask about any suspicious characters who might have been seen in the neighbourhood. Two rough-looking men had been lurking in the vicinity and were at once suspected, but when Superintendent Phelps of Chipping Sodbury arrived he felt at once that this was not a random killing. Local enquiries soon revealed that Scott had last been seen with William Williams, and the police went to the Priory, where PC Brown searched the coat William had left lying on the floor. In its pocket he found a six-chambered revolver, one chamber of which had been discharged.

About the same time that Richings was finding the body of Scott, Marshall Williams, unable to get back to sleep after his disturbed night, got up and began to pack his things. It was then he noticed that his revolver, a loaded, heavy-calibre Smith and Wesson, which he usually carried in a satchel, was missing. He at once felt certain that his brother had taken it to kill himself, especially as William had more than once before threatened to commit suicide. Despite this conclusion he seemed to feel no great sense of urgency. The obvious thing to do was to alert the police and hurry to see his brother. Instead, Marshall said nothing to the police or anyone else about his concerns for his brother's life, but finished packing his things and then ate breakfast before going to Batt's Hotel. The porter showed Marshall up to his brother's room, where, assuming that the door was locked ('for if a man wants to commit suicide he generally locks the door'), he first knocked and then called out his brother's name. Receiving no response, he hammered more loudly on the woodwork. The *Stroud News* later added its own touch of drama to the story by stating that the door was locked and had to be

SUICIDE OF THE SUSPECT IN A WEST END HOTEL.

TERRIBLE CRIME IN GLOUCESTERSHIRE,
CYCLIST FOULLY MURDERED ON THE COTSWOLD HILLS.

The body is found. (*Illustrated Police News*, 23 August 1902)

forced, but, as Marshall later reported, when he tried the handle he found the door unlocked, and he simply walked in. William was in bed, lying on his left side. He was naked, his clothes were scattered in disarray all around the room and he was very obviously dead. The pool of blood on the bed was so large that Marshall thought at first that his brother had shot himself in the heart. On closer inspection he saw that there was a gaping wound in the forehead, from which blood had poured profusely. Blood had also flowed from the nose, covering the shoulders and chest and saturating the bedclothes. The revolver had fallen from William's lifeless hand and lay on the floor. Marshall, who seems to have taken matters calmly, felt the body, and found it still soft on the outside but with an internal rigidity which suggested that William had been dead for some hours. He looked through his brother's clothes, removed his pocket book and a sovereign, then rang the bell and asked to see the manager. It so happened that the hotel was run by a manageress. This lady presented herself, but in view of the seriousness of the situation Marshall said he preferred to see a man. There was a further delay while a manager from another hotel was sent for, and when he arrived Marshall reported his brother's suicide, and said that he was going down to the country and would come back at 3 p.m. to see the police. He said nothing about William's claim to have killed John Scott. The hotel reported the matter to the Vine Street police station, and the police and Dr Mitchell, the divisional police surgeon, were called to the scene, where William Williams was pronounced dead. The body was removed to a mortuary, where Dr Mitchell later made a post-mortem examination. He saw that the skin of the forehead was blackened by the discharge of the pistol, and the hair just above it was singed. He had no doubt that the wound was self-inflicted. Inspector Drew of the CID informed the Gloucestershire County Constabulary of William Williams's death, and it was only then that the vital connection was made between the suicide and the recent discovery of Scott's body.

Marshall had in the meantime checked out of his own hotel and gone to Sevenoaks, where he telegraphed 'Mr Knocker' (either Evelyn's brother Reginald or her uncle William – which, he did not specify) to meet him at Sevenoaks

SUICIDE OF THE SUSPECT IN A WEST END HOTEL.

Suicide of Williams in a West End hotel. (Illustrated Police News, 23 August 1902)

station. His uncertainty about the fate of John Scott, which had prevented him from taking any action on the previous night or saying anything to the police, seemed to have vanished, for on meeting with the Knocker family he told them that his brother had killed John Scott. He then accompanied Evelyn and Mr and Mrs Knocker back to Stroud, where he learned that Scott's body had been found, and here he was finally obliged to make a statement to the police.

John Scott's body had been taken to the Barley Mow Inn, Hawkesbury Upton, to await the inquest, which opened on Saturday 16 August, but only Richings and Forty gave evidence. Dr Forty stated that Scott was 5ft 11in tall and weighed 13 stone, so that the person who disposed of the body must have had enormous strength, and so he theorised that two persons might have been involved. There was, however, good evidence that the body had been dragged by the heels, and it was a juryman who made the good point that, had there been two men, the body would have been carried. The *Stroud Journal* later stated that according to those who knew him Scott was of spare build and 5ft 8in tall. This strange discrepancy was not resolved by the press. The inquest was adjourned, and it was not until the following day that Reginald Knocker arrived at the Barley Mow and formally identified his brother-in-law's body, after which it was removed to the Priory.

The inquest on William Williams was held on Monday 18 August at Horseferry Road, Westminster. Williams, stated Dr Mitchell, was in good health and had died of shock consequent on a bullet entering his brain. The chief witness and object of a great deal of scrutiny was Marshall Bruce Williams, who was then residing at the Hotel Metropole. Marshall said that, as far as he was aware, his brother and Scott were the best of friends. He had never seen any trouble between them, and neither had he seen any disagreement between Mr and Mrs Scott. Questioned as to why he had not reported his brother's confession to anyone, he said that he knew some of his brother's statements to be unreliable and 'I did not know whether Mr Scott was only slightly injured or dead', a comment that entirely failed to explain his lack of urgency. He admitted that following William's confession of murder the sole advice he had given his brother was to go to bed. Asked to comment on his brother's mental condition, he said that William 'was a very unhappy and unfortunate man. He had often threatened to commit suicide.' He also said that there had been great differences between William and their father. He believed that William had not been of sound mind for some months, and had been wondering if he should not be put into professional care. Mr Troutbeck, the coroner, commented in summing up that the conduct of the brother had been 'of a very unusual character. This extraordinary secrecy at such a time was ill-judged.' At this, some of the jurymen, who were probably expressing the views of all present, called out 'Hear, hear.' It was impossible, went on Troutbeck, to assign any reason for the conduct of the man, who could not himself be a suspect. It was fortunate, he hinted, that there was another person present when the body was found.

The jury found a verdict of 'Suicide while temporarily insane' but wanted to add an unusual rider – the comment that the brother of the deceased was deserving of

Williams hides his friend's body. (Illustrated Police News, 23 August 1902)

censure. The coroner disapproved of this, as the case was still *sub judice*. The foreman of the jury said it was their opinion that the brother ought to have prevented the suicide. 'There is no evidence on that point,' said Troutbeck. 'The jury thought', persisted the foreman, 'if the brother had followed the deceased he would have prevented him committing suicide.' No one seems to have disagreed.

Whatever William's mental state he could hardly have chosen a better spot for murder. It was wholly unsurprising that no one had heard the report of the pistol or interrupted either the deed or its concealment. Even if the shot had been heard the shooting of rabbits and vermin was a common practice in the area, and no one would have given it any thought. The two men must have been cycling past the gate to Saddlewood Farm, with William, who was right-handed, a little behind and to the left of Scott, when he had taken out the pistol and shot his companion, who died instantly. From the mud-stained appearance of William's cycling clothes, it was later believed that he had not cycled back to the Priory on the main road but had taken another, semi-private route, climbing gates and carrying his bicycle over several fields on the way.

The only mystery was the motive. After the tragic events the newspapers were full of speculation about why William Williams had suddenly shot his best friend. It was widely rumoured that the men had been heard quarrelling at the Priory, though both the servants denied having heard anything, and Mrs Scott was silent on the subject. Another rumour was that William had conceived a great passion for Mrs Scott, which he had not revealed to her but had confessed all to Scott during a quarrel. The result of this, said the newspapers, was a cooling off of the friendship, an estrangement between the families and William being ordered out of the Priory by his erstwhile friend. Mrs Scott, it was suggested, was not merely on holiday but, annoyed at William constantly following her about the house and garden, had gone away with the children to avoid him, telling her husband she expected him to be gone on her return. The only problem with this theory was that to all outward appearances Scott and William were, shortly before the murder, on terms of great amity, continuing to dine and take companionable bicycle rides together. William's feelings for Mrs Scott must have been in some way associated with the murder, since at his last interview with his brother he clearly stated that his action was the best thing for her. He had told Marshall that there were disagreements between the couple, with legal action being contemplated, and that Scott had not treated his wife kindly and had once even threatened her with a revolver, something the Knocker family, on behalf of the distraught Evelyn, later hotly denied. 'The rumours', said her father, Sir E. Wollaston Knocker, were 'cruel and untrue and cowardly and unkind . . . . No one would repudiate them more strongly than my daughter's husband, were he alive.' No proof regarding the allegations was ever forthcoming, and they could well have emanated only from the disturbed mind of William Williams. It was true that shortly before the murder William had been irritable and distracted and given to sudden bursts of temper, but whether this was from any real cause or a symptom of his obsession is a matter for speculation.

On 19 August Horsley was filled with people arriving from the surrounding towns and villages to witness the funeral of John Dudley Scott. The body was borne from the Priory to the church just 100 yards away, the two buildings being separated only by an apple orchard. The oak coffin bore the simple inscription, 'John Dudley Scott, born October 22nd 1874, died August 14th 1902.' Members of both the Scott and Knocker families were present, as well as local gentry, but Mrs Scott was too prostrated with grief to attend. She remained at the Priory, where her children were seen playing, innocently unaware of the tragic reason for the sudden influx of visitors. She sent a wreath of white flowers in the form of a cross, which was placed upon the coffin. As the remains were laid to rest the pretty churchyard was lashed by a sudden summer storm, dark clouds and rolling thunder providing a fitting backdrop to the unhappy scene.

A rumour had been going around Horsley that William Williams was to be buried in the same churchyard, where his mother Eliza was already buried. Having attended the funeral of Scott a substantial crowd of protesters gathered in the orchard and around the churchyard gates, determined to prevent the funeral of the murderer so close to his victim. The clouds had drifted away, and the village was now illuminated by the harvest moon. 'We ain't agoin' to have it,' declared a sturdy individual named Hodge. 'The Major's wife is buried there but if they try to bury the son agen her and the murdered man we'll stop the ceremony.' It was explained to the crowd that any plans to bury William Williams

St Martin's Church, Horsley. (Author's collection)

The spot where the body of Mr. Dudley Scott was found.
(The cross shows where the body was dragged over the wall after being brought through the gateway. The circle marks the spot where the bicycle was found.)

The spot where the body was found. Contemporary sketch. (Daily Graphic, 20 August 1902)

in Horsley had been abandoned, and the villagers eventually dispersed down the hill along the moonlit roadway. The funeral of William Wright Williams was held the following day at Kensal Green cemetery. The only mourner was his brother.

On 22 August the inquest on John Scott resumed at the Assembly Rooms, Hawkesbury Upton. Marshall Williams gave evidence, and the natural curiosity of the jury led to questions about the death of his brother which the coroner told him not to answer. Marshall said he was anxious to clarify matters because of things said in the newspapers. 'I never listen to what is in the papers because they tell all sorts of lies,' growled the coroner, Dr Grace. 'If I had a sovereign for every lie that has been told about me I should not want to work again.' The jury had no difficulty in returning a verdict of wilful murder against William Wright Williams. The *Stroud News* later commented that the tragedy was the first case where a bicycle had played such a prominent part in a drama of that character: 'fact has outstripped fiction by introducing the bicycle with its powers of noiseless stealthy approach as a lethal agent'.

The Priory eventually passed into the hands of Gloucestershire County Council, but today it is a beautiful and welcoming guest house, which still preserves its secrets of the strange death of John Dudley Scott.

8

THE POISONING OF HARRY PACE

Fetter Hill, near Coleford, 1928

The Forest of Dean in west Gloucestershire has a long industrial history, founded on coal seams, deposits of iron ore and outcrops of limestone, supported by the oak timber of its ancient woodlands. The town of Coleford, a thriving settlement since at least the thirteenth century, has been a centre of mining, smelting and quarrying for most of its history.

In 1924 a married couple, Beatrice and Harry Pace, came to live in a three-room cottage on the edge of Coleford, just a few yards off the main road from Fetter Hill to Sling. Harry Pace was a quarryman, but in common with many other men in the area he supplemented his wages by keeping a flock of sheep, pasturing them on the wastes and verges of the Forest of Dean. He would get up at 4 a.m. each day to tend to the sheep before going to the quarry, then go to look after the sheep again on his return from work.

Beatrice Pace was born Beatrice Annie Martin in St Briavels in 1889. A shepherd's daughter, she left school shortly before she was 12 to look after her sick mother,

Mrs Beatrice Pace. (Associated Newspapers)

who died not long afterwards. She did not return to school but stayed at home until she was 14, when she went to London to go into domestic service. By then she had met Harry Pace, a quarryman's son of Ellwood, who was a year her junior, and they used to write to each other. When she came home they 'walked out' and were married in 1909 in the register office at Monmouth. In nineteen years of marriage Beatrice gave birth to ten children, only five of whom were still living in 1928: 17-year-old Dorothy, Doris, 11, Leslie, 10, Selwyn (sometimes called Teddy), 6, and the baby, Jean.

While Harry Pace's relatives would afterwards state that the marriage had been a happy one and he had been very kind to his wife, both Mrs Pace and her children told a different tale. Harry Pace was subject to violent fits of temper and erratic behaviour, and often beat his wife. Once he tied her to the bed and left her there all day long, only untying her when he came home from work. After a savage beating with a wire rope she had fled to her father's house. Harry pursued her with a pistol in his hand, threatening to shoot her. On another occasion he had forced her head on to the table and tried to strike her with a hatchet. In 1924 she formally summonsed him for beating her, and he was bound over in the sum of £10. Animals did not escape his fury. When one of his sheep was killed on the railway line he exploded in anger, picking up Beatrice's dog, a little Pomeranian, and dashing its brains out against a wall. He was also cruel to his sheep and dogs, sometimes kicking them and biting their ears. His mood swings were terrifying, ranging from days spent in sullen silence to episodes of slapping his sides and crowing like a cockerel or barking like a dog, or scratching his head till it bled and his hair came out. Early in 1927 Harry turned his wife and children out of the house, threatening to shoot them, and Beatrice reported the incident to the local police. Sergeant Hamblin of Coleford police station was sent to speak to Harry about it. In March 1927, when Beatrice was six months pregnant with their tenth child, Harry beat her with a walking stick.

Harry was also notorious as a sexual predator, many of his victims being girls as young as 12 – one of them Beatrice's sister Florence, who had had to be sent away from home. In November 1926 Beatrice had received a letter from the parents of a Miss Childs of Marsh Lane, saying they were going to summons Harry for indecent assault. Harry asked Beatrice to give them 7s 6d (38p) to say no more about it. She paid up. On another occasion a heavily pregnant Beatrice had come home early and found Harry behind the front door with a Miss Scholesberg of Bream, the arrangement of their clothing leaving nothing to the imagination. She went to see the girl's parents, who were going to take Harry to court but took pity on Beatrice because of her condition. They did nothing.

It may well have been that Harry's family knew nothing of, or turned a blind eye to, his violence and womanising, and they were deeply offended when Beatrice said harsh things about her husband. Harry's married sister Leah Pritchard, brothers Leonard and Elton Pace, and Leonard's wife Gertrude were all later to express their dislike and distrust of Beatrice. According to them, Beatrice sometimes said she wished Harry would come home from work stiff, called him a 'mingey old bugger' and said she would like to poison him. The family also suspected Beatrice of affairs with other men. Near neighbour Leslie Sayes, whose wife Alice was a close friend of Beatrice's, was a frequent visitor when Harry was at work, and Elton, who often came to the house and found the man there, had rowed with Beatrice about this. Both Sayes and Beatrice denied that anything was going on, and Alice Sayes firmly refused to believe it.

No one had any evidence of adultery against Beatrice, but Leah had once visited the cottage to be told by Doris that her mother wasn't in. Leah had pushed the door open and saw her sister-in-law in a room looking 'very flustrated [*sic*] and dishevelled'.

At the end of May 1927 Harry Pace and his wife both visited their doctor, William Henry Du Pre, of Rosewarne, Coleford. Harry was complaining of stomach pains and occasional vomiting of blood. He was diagnosed with either a gastric ulcer or gastritis and prescribed bismuth and soda. There was some improvement, but towards the end of June his condition suddenly worsened and there were symptoms of paralysis in his hands and feet. Du Pre saw him regularly throughout the summer.

On 22 July Beatrice purchased two packets of sheep dip from the local chemist. These packets were stored in a wooden box which the family called the 'sheep box'. On 23 July Harry and Beatrice used one of the packets to dip sixteen lambs. Leslie helped with the work, and Doris and Teddy were also there. The lambs were dipped in a small 'dolly tub' about 50 yards from the house. Harry mixed the dip in a bucket and then filled the tub. Each lamb was lifted into the tub and

Centre of Coleford, 1910. (Author's collection)

pushed into the liquid with his bare hands. It was a day or two later before he emptied the remaining liquid from the tub. Not all the powdered dip was used, so the rest was wrapped in paper and put in the sheep box with the other full packet. The adult sheep were due to be dipped the following month.

Within days Harry Pace was again taken ill. He had gone to work taking with him a breakfast of bread and butter, cake and tea, all of which Beatrice had prepared. When he returned home he complained of pains in the stomach and head, and vomiting.

Elton Pace visited his brother and was alarmed to find him in bed, hunched up in pain with his knees to his stomach. Beatrice was lying across her husband's chest, exclaiming, 'Harry, Harry, you be dying! We shall not see you much longer!' Elton thought her weight was impeding Harry's breath, so he grabbed her by the back of the neck and pulled her off.

Harry's mother, Mrs Elizabeth Porter, a widow who had remarried, also visited, and found her son complaining of sickness and bad stomach pains. Suspicious that he was not being cared for properly, she wanted to be left alone with him to ask if he was 'being done right by', but Beatrice was always there. When Harry complained of thirst Mrs Porter gave him some water from a cup on a box by the bed, but he was unable to drink it. She tried it and found it had a peculiar taste, so she brought fresh water, which he drank gratefully.

On 28 July George Mountjoy, a schoolteacher, was asked to go to the Paces' house, where he assisted Harry in making a will in which everything was left to Beatrice. The estate consisted of the sheep, of which there were over eighty, some farm tools and the furniture. There was in addition a policy on Harry's life, taken out in 1924, which would pay £69 12s (£69.60) on his death (worth about £2,600 today). With Harry ill in bed Leslie Sayes helped look after the sheep, and Mrs Sayes sometimes helped attend the sick man.

By August Harry had no sense of touch in his hands and feet and had lost power in his limbs. He was unable to stand when he got out of bed. Mrs Porter wanted a second doctor called in, but Beatrice objected, claiming it would be too expensive. It was Leonard Pace who paid two guineas for the consultation, and Dr Ram Nath Nanda of St Briavels called on 11 August, together with Dr Du Pre. Beatrice had sent notes to Leonard, Elton and Mrs Porter saying that the doctors would be there at 1.30 p.m., but suspecting that she might have deliberately given the wrong time Elton kept a watch outside the house, and Mrs Porter was also there early. Their suspicions were correct – the two doctors arrived at 11.30 a.m. At 11.50 a.m. Elton looked in and saw Beatrice with Du Pre and a nurse, Mrs Kear, Dr Nanda being upstairs examining Harry. Elton called Beatrice outside and demanded to know what she meant by giving him the wrong time. She called him a bully and said, 'I don't want to see you or any of the family down here!' He called her 'a bloody liar' and stormed off.

The doctors agreed that Harry Pace should go to hospital, and he was taken to Gloucester Infirmary on 19 August. He was unable to walk and had to be carried in. There the resident medical officer, Dr Mather, theorised that Harry was suffering from arsenical poisoning caused by exposure to sheep dip. A fellow patient was Charles Fletcher, who had known Harry for about fifteen years. Harry was very depressed about his condition and told Fletcher he didn't think he would recover. Another patient, Arthur Smith, saw him crying, and once or twice Harry told Smith that if he got no better he would 'do himself in'. Mrs Pace sometimes visited, bringing her husband cakes, which he shared with Smith.

That month Harry asked his brother Leonard to dip his sheep for him, which Leonard did on 27 August, but he did not use his brother's supply of sheep dip, as another man had already mixed some.

Harry was eager to get home and left hospital on 24 October. He was still unable to walk and had to be carried out, the ward sister commenting that he was very foolish to leave. Du Pre visited Harry; though the stomach symptoms had cleared up, the man seemed weaker than when he had gone into hospital and was still unable to stand without support. Against expectation, however, Du Pre observed on his regular visits that Harry's condition was steadily improving. Did Harry suspect he had been poisoned by the powdered sheep dip? Shortly after his return from hospital, on a day when Beatrice was out in Coleford, he took out the sheep box, had a look at the paper-wrapped packet, returned it to the box and asked Leslie to put it away in the chest of drawers in the bedroom.

A fortnight after Harry left hospital Charles Fletcher came to visit him and found him much improved, although Harry said that the doctor had told him he wouldn't be able to get about again for two years. It had by now been confirmed that he was suffering from arsenical poisoning, although he had no idea how he had got it, as he did not think he had been careless with the sheep dip. Another visitor, who had come at the request of Mrs Porter, was Fred Thorne, a miner who had some skill in massage. When Harry came out of hospital, despondent and miserable, Thorne went regularly to Fetter Hill to treat him and over the weeks saw a steady improvement. In November Dorothy, who had been in domestic service in Hereford, returned home and found her father still spending much of his time in bed. He remained depressed about his illness, and several times she heard him say that he wished he could get something to finish himself off. A fortnight before Christmas, however, Harry was telling Leonard he felt much better, and by Christmas-time he was able to walk about unaided.

On Christmas Day Dorothy was laying a fire in the grate of her father's bedroom when she noticed a bottle in the fender. She took it out and put it on the chest of drawers, and told her mother about it. Beatrice went upstairs and asked Harry what the bottle was for, but he denied knowing anything about it.

Harry Pace was in a bad mood that day. It was too cold in the bedroom, so he dressed and came downstairs to sit morosely by the fire. Suddenly he seized the fire tongs and went to hit Beatrice with them, yelling, 'I will knock your bloody brains out!' He only desisted when Dorothy stood in front of her mother. Angrily he began to beat in the fireguard instead. Throwing down the tongs, he took a razor from a cupboard, and at this Beatrice sent Doris to run to a neighbour's house and fetch help.

'Clear out or I'll kill the bloody lot of you!' threatened Harry, and Beatrice and Dorothy both rushed out of the house. They returned when he had calmed down. Beatrice asked him what the matter was, and he asked her to forgive him. When Doris came back with Reginald Martin, a baker of Lower Milkwall, whose house was only some 200–300 yards away, Harry was sitting calmly by the fireside with a blanket wrapped around him, as if nothing had happened. Dorothy whispered to Martin that she had found a bottle in the fireplace and thought her father might have taken something. Martin could do little more than try to persuade Harry that he ought to go up to bed. That night Harry was taken violently ill again.

On Boxing Day Beatrice ran round to Dr Du Pre and said that Harry was 'awfully bad'. Du Pre sent round some medicine. When he saw Harry the next day he found the patient in bed with stomach pains and vomiting after meals. Du Pre diagnosed gastric flu and ordered a milk-and-water diet and some white of egg.

There were many visits to the cottage during Harry's illness. Leonard Pace called on Boxing Day, when Harry said he was not feeling so well, commenting unhappily that three days before he had been able to walk about the room. Two days later Thorne called and saw that Harry was very ill. On 3 January Charles Fletcher saw Harry groaning and retching and rolling about on the bed. Beatrice gave her husband brandy and water, but he couldn't keep it down. Three days later Fletcher called again and found Harry virtually helpless, almost in a daze. By the time Dr Du Pre visited on 8 January Harry was taking very little nourishment. Beatrice prepared a cup of cornflour and milk and placed it beside the bed, but whether he was able to drink any was later disputed.

Fred Thorne saw Harry again on 9 January, when Harry said weakly what a shame it was to 'go back' like that after he had improved so much. He complained of a thumping in his head, and his heart was beating terribly. Beatrice again went to fetch Dr Du Pre, who found his patient prostrate, with pains in the head, stomach and throat. Harry was able to take only the white of an egg with a little brandy. Elton arrived but Beatrice tried to get him to leave, saying her husband was having diarrhoea. She was rushing up and down the stairs, tending to the sick man, and Elton could hear his brother retching. After 20 minutes Elton went upstairs and found Harry doubled up with pain, only just able to turn on his side to vomit into the 'Jeremiah' under the bed.

On 10 January Fletcher again visited Harry. He found him in great pain and panting heavily. Beatrice, Mrs Sayes and Mrs Kear were present. Elton arrived at 11 a.m. and thought his brother was near to death. He stayed only two minutes before going to fetch Dr Du Pre. Gradually Harry lapsed into unconsciousness and died. Leah Pritchard later claimed that she was present that day and that she saw Harry die in great agony, but Mrs Sayes denied that Leah was there and said that Harry had passed away peacefully after being unconscious for the last hour. Dr Du Pre certified death as due to influenza, gastroenteritis, peripheral neuritis (an inflammation of the nerves of the extremities) and anuria (cessation of urine production).

On the following day Elton Pace went to Coleford police station, and told Inspector Alan Bent that the family was not satisfied that Harry had died from natural causes. Bent questioned other members of the family and found them similarly unhappy. He called on Beatrice, who made a statement saying that the rumours were untrue. He asked her if there was any sheep dip in the house. She took a full packet of Battle's sheep dip out of the cupboard. Asked if there was any left from the dipping of the lambs, she said there was not and thought the packet had probably been burned. Rumours began to spread around the neighbourhood suggesting not only that Beatrice had poisoned her husband but that Leslie Sayes had helped her do it, with Mrs Sayes presumably the next victim in line.

The funeral of Harry Pace was due to take place on 15 January but was stopped by order of the police. On 13 January Sergeant Hamblin and Inspector Bent called on Beatrice to tell her that a post-mortem examination would have to be carried out, and she mentioned for the first time the bottle in the fender of the bedroom. 'I do not know whether he drank any of it, but several times he has told me he was tired of life and threatened to commit suicide,' she said. Beatrice then made a formal statement, describing her violent and unhappy marriage.

The post-mortem was conducted at the Pace cottage on 14 January by Dr Carson of Lydney, who gave the cause of death as arsenical poisoning. Inspector Bent was present and took the opportunity to have a look around and remove any bottles or powders that might have contained arsenic. The most obvious source of arsenic in the house was sheep dip. Manufactured since 1852, powdered sheep dip was a bright-yellow preparation of arsenic and sulphur. One packet, when mixed with 20 gallons of water, was enough to dip about twenty sheep, and eighteen teaspoonfuls of this solution would contain two grains – a potentially fatal dose. The dry powder was about 21 per cent arsenic, 65 per cent sulphur. One packet contained about 1,400 fatal doses.

Following the post-mortem, a number of jars containing some of Harry Pace's organs and some samples of skin and bone were given to Mr R.H. Ellis, the county analyst. The total amount of arsenic found in the organs was 9.42 grains.

The inquest on Harry Pace opened at Coleford Court House on 16 January before Mr M.F. Carter, coroner for the Forest of Dean, and was at once adjourned. After the hearing Inspector Bent noticed that Mrs Pace was on the verge of collapse and had her taken home. The newspapers reported that there she lapsed into unconsciousness, and the doctors who were summoned were unable to revive her. She was still said to be unconscious by the evening, a condition that was attributed to severe shock. Beatrice was to exhibit a tendency to collapse in a faint at dramatic moments many times over the next few months.

On 17 January the body of Harry Pace was buried in the small cemetery in the nearby village of Clearwell. Beatrice was too ill to attend.

George Mountjoy, executor of Pace's will, was not informed of Harry's death, but when he did find out he discovered that Beatrice's sole means of support was about £3 worth of tools and just nine sheep. The rest of the flock had been sold

Clearwell cemetery. (Author's collection)

by Beatrice during Harry's illness. He at once put a stop to any more sales being made out of the estate.

Police investigations continued over the next few weeks, during which Beatrice was asked to make further statements. Frustrated at the slow workings of the law, Elton Pace decided to follow Leslie Sayes as he was on his way home on 23 February and shouted out to him that he was a murderer. 'Armstrong!' he yelled, a reference to the notorious poisoner of Hay on Wye. He also openly accused Sayes of having an affair with Beatrice. Sayes was obliged to make a complaint to the police and see his solicitor about the continuing nuisance.

Eventually Scotland Yard was called in and on 7 March arrived in the person of Chief Inspector Cornish and Detective Sergeant Campion, who proceeded to interrogate a large number of people. On 11 March Beatrice was brought to the police station with Doris and Leslie. Both the children were questioned, and Beatrice made a long statement. She revealed that in addition to her ten pregnancies she had had two miscarriages.

Cornish saw her again three days later, when she handed him a letter as well as a small tin containing some tablets, which she said her husband had given to her saying, 'If you are tired of life, take one of them. You will soon —— well, die.' That evening she came to Coleford where another statement was taken. Beatrice now said that both her miscarriages had been procured by Harry who, when she was two or three months pregnant, had placed a lump of some unknown substance into her 'private part' and then 'had connection' with her. In both cases she had miscarried a few days later. She had also found herself pregnant within a few weeks of Harry's returning from hospital and had taken 'medicines and injections which cleared me'. Finally she admitted that she had lied to the police when she had told them she had never been with another man. She had 'had connections' with a man called Stanley Dominey. Her statement done, Beatrice complained of feeling unwell and fainted. She was taken home in a car.

The inquest resumed in March. It was to run to fourteen hearings in all, Mr Trevor Wellington appearing for Mrs Pace. When she took her place in court, dressed dramatically in deep mourning, a screen was placed between her and the public.

Elton Pace testified that Beatrice had complained about her husband's meanness, saying she wished she was single and never wanted to marry again. He asserted that Beatrice had several times said she would 'poison the old bugger'.

When Leah Pritchard spoke of Harry's agonising death Beatrice showed signs of faintness and was helped out of the court by a policewoman and Mrs Sayes. Leah was a woman of very decided opinions. She asserted, contrary to almost everyone else, that Harry had returned home from hospital better than when he had been admitted. She declared that she had never known her brother threaten to take his own life: 'He was a man most anxious to live.' Asked if she was on friendly terms with Mrs Pace, Leah said, 'Nothing has been between us except that I did not visit her house.' Asked why this was, she said, 'For reasons of my own; for my own respectability.'

'Was your real reason that you thought she was associating with other men?' demanded the coroner, to which she simply said, 'Yes.'

Mr Wellington read out a statement from a hospital patient stating that Harry had been better able to move about and do things for himself when he arrived in hospital than when he left it. 'That is news to me,' said Mrs Pritchard. The same patient, continued Wellington, had also said that Harry had said he couldn't bear to be a cripple all his life and would sooner commit suicide. Mrs Pritchard said firmly that she didn't believe it.

Dorothy Pace said that in November the family had been happy, but admitted that her father had been violent and said she had no affection for him because of his cruelty. The court may well have gained the impression that the only reason the household had been so peaceable in November was that her father was ill in bed. Ten-year-old Doris was even blunter. 'Were you happy at home?' the coroner asked her. 'No,' she replied. 'Why not?' Doris explained, 'Because Dad threatened to kill us all. He had a bad temper and said he would take his life.'

Although several witnesses stated that Harry Pace had talked of suicide, it is noticeable that these comments were all made when he was very seriously ill, suffering from agonising pain, sickness and paralysis. It was not a surprising thing to say under the circumstances, but it is impossible to know how seriously he meant it.

Opposite: *Sketches from the* Illustrated Police News. (*Illustrated Police News*, 1928)

July 12, 1928.   **THE ILLUSTRATED POLICE NEWS**   5

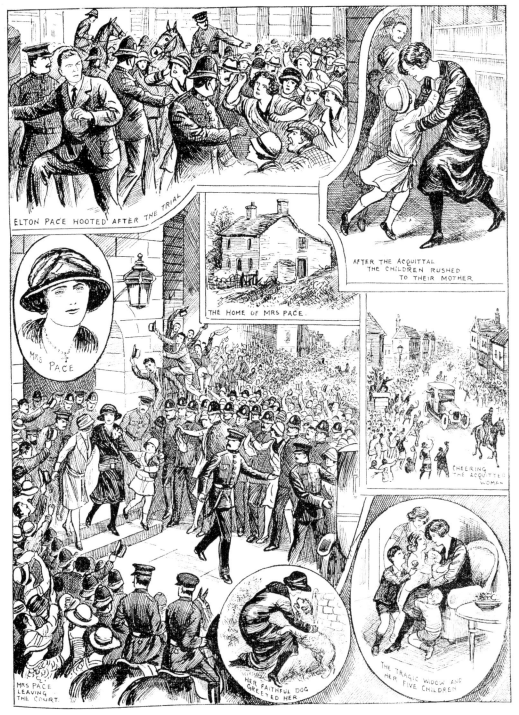

ELTON PACE HOOTED AFTER THE TRIAL

AFTER THE ACQUITTAL THE CHILDREN RUSHED TO THEIR MOTHER

THE HOME OF MRS PACE.

MRS PACE

CHEERING THE ACQUITTED WOMAN

MRS PACE LEAVING THE COURT.

HER FAITHFUL DOG GREETED HER.

THE TRAGIC WIDOW AND HER FIVE CHILDREN

REMARKABLE SCENES AFTER THE ACQUITTAL OF MRS. PACE.

Mrs Sayes, meanwhile, was adamant that there had been nothing between her husband and Mrs Pace. She had heard the rumour and questioned both parties, but she was satisfied that it was untrue. 'And what is more, sir, I do not believe it of my husband. He is not built that way.'

Doctors Du Pre and Nanda both testified that peripheral neuritis was a well-known symptom of arsenical poisoning, which both were now certain was the cause of death, though Nanda added that he did not believe it was possible to absorb enough arsenic though the skin to cause this symptom. None of the medicines prescribed to Harry during his illness, including those given to him at hospital, contained arsenic.

Dr Ellis testified on 11 May. At the first mention of the jars he had examined Beatrice was overcome with emotion and had to be assisted from the court. In the witness box Ellis demonstrated that if sheep dip was shaken up with water it left a yellow sulphurous sediment, with a colourless liquid on top which contained the arsenic. This clear solution had no smell and only a slightly salty taste. It could be mixed with tea, or milk and cornflour, or egg white. A dusty bottle found on the Paces' kitchen shelf contained a solution of sheep dip in which the sulphur had settled as a sediment, the clear liquid containing traces of arsenic, coloured purple with potassium permanganate, a disinfectant. Mrs Pace had denied knowing anything about it.

Professor Isaac Walker Hall, pathologist of Bristol University, testified that arsenic had been taken by Harry Pace over a period of at least fourteen to twenty-one days and perhaps for up to four to six months. He agreed that it was possible for arsenic to be absorbed through the skin, but only if there was a cut or abrasion. He added that the solution used for sheep dipping contained only 0.2 per cent of arsenic, and he did not believe it possible for anyone to absorb sufficient through the skin to cause illness.

Sir William Willcox, medical advisor to the Home Office, stated that the quantities of arsenic found in the body were consistent with Pace having taken a large dose within forty-eight hours of his death, though not within the six hours preceding. A large dose had probably been taken on the day of onset of the serious symptoms in July, and a dose must have been taken just before the onset of symptoms on Christmas Day. He believed that a number of other doses had been taken between Christmas Day and the day of death. He declared that Harry could not have been poisoned by absorbing arsenic through the skin, unless there was a very extensive wound, of which there was no evidence.

On 15 May the screen was removed and Beatrice was called to give evidence amid very considerable excitement in court. She denied having given her husband poison. Although there were rumours that there was a great deal of money in the house, she said that the most she ever knew about was £7, which was spent when the baby was born the previous June. There had been 8s 6d (43p) arrears on the insurance policy, which she had paid the night before Harry died. She was in the witness box for two and a half hours when the coroner adjourned so she could have a cup of tea. On resumption Beatrice claimed that about a week or fortnight before Christmas Harry had cried nearly all the afternoon, saying he would never be any good to her or the children. He had gone to the window to throw himself out, but she got hold of him and made him go back to bed. He had, she said, threatened to kill himself on many occasions. Asked how she thought the arsenic had got in to her husband's body, she said 'I cannot tell you, I cannot tell you.'

On 22 May the coroner's jury met for the fourteenth time, and Mr Carter summed up. He said there was nothing to support the view that Harry Pace had died from an accident. On the question of suicide, he pointed out that Harry had endured considerable pain over a long period of time, and asked, 'Is it conceivable that a man is going to dose himself with arsenic from July 1927 down to January 10 in order to bring about his own death?' Who, he asked the jury pointedly, had the opportunity to prepare the man's food and drink, and administer his medicine?

The jury was out for an hour, after which they announced that they had reached a unanimous verdict. 'We find that Harry Pace met his death at Fetter Hill on January 10 by arsenical poisoning administered by some person or persons other than himself. We are agreed that the case calls for further investigation.'

To their surprise, the coroner told them that this would not do. It was necessary for them to name a person or persons, so that further enquiry could be made. The foreman said that the jury was not agreed on this point, and the court was cleared so they could reconsider their verdict. When the hearing resumed, the jury declared that they had found that Harry Pace had met his death by poison administered by Beatrice Pace. Beatrice at once became hysterical and, after being taken to the police station below, swooned away. When she recovered she was charged with murder and taken to Cardiff prison.

Beatrice appeared before Coleford magistrates on 29 May for the first of several days of proceedings, during which her statements about her violent marriage were read to the court. On 4 June she was committed for trial. She at once fainted away in the dock and had to be carried from the court.

The trial opened at Gloucester Assizes on 2 July before Mr Justice Horridge. The case had achieved nationwide publicity, and there was almost universal sympathy for Beatrice. Special police were placed on duty outside the Shire Hall, where those who could not gain admission to the crowded court had gathered. Appearing for Mrs Pace was Norman Birkett (later Lord Birkett, and a distinguished High Court Judge).

In his questioning of Mrs Porter, Harry's mother, Birkett tried to reveal her animosity towards Beatrice, and then, to bolster the suggestion that Harry had committed suicide, tried to show that there was insanity in the family. Mrs Porter was obliged to admit that she had had an illegitimate son in 1908, but when Birkett revealed that this son had shot himself while of unsound mind, it transpired, embarrassingly, that this was the first Mrs Porter knew of it.

By the third day of the trial Beatrice was being cheered by the crowds when she arrived at the Shire Hall. Dr Du Pre testified that on 2 December the loving wife had walked 3 miles to his surgery through snow that was higher than her knees.

Elton Pace made a poor showing in the witness box. His evidence about his relationship with Beatrice was vague and contradictory, and he eventually retreated into claiming that he couldn't remember things as he had a lot on his plate. He then made the mistake of trying to cast doubt on the evidence given by the medical men.

When Beatrice left the court the crowds were so large that mounted police had to be called in to keep order. As the car carrying the prisoner passed by there was an outburst of cheering, men waved their caps and women leaned out of windows to wave handkerchiefs. Public sympathy increased when on the fourth day Beatrice's statement about her husband's cruelty and infidelity was read out in court.

On day five the prosecution case was completed by lunchtime, and after the recess Mr Birkett submitted that there was no case to put before the jury, in that the evidence was consistent with self-administration as much as with any other theory, and there was no evidence of administration by the accused. Mr Justice Horridge concluded that it would not be safe to continue with the case, directing the jury to return a formal verdict of 'not guilty'. It was an emotional moment, but this time Beatrice did not faint. Dazed at first, she rose to shake hands with Mr

Opposite: *Norman Birkett KC, MP, c. 1929.* (Westminster Press Provincial Newspapers)

Right: Mrs Pace and Doris after the trial. (*Daily Mail*)

Birkett, and this was the signal for a great outburst of cheering. Emerging from the Shire Hall, she briefly acknowledged the cheers of the crowd, then waved her hands and blew kisses as she was driven away. Birkett was also cheered by the crowds, but members of the Pace family had to face a storm of booing.

When the news reached Coleford there was great excitement and crowds gathered outside the King's Head Hotel, where Beatrice arrived at 5 p.m. to have tea. She stayed there one night before going away in the company of Mrs Sayes for a one week holiday in Windsor. Soon afterwards the friendly relationship between Beatrice and the Sayes family was in ruins. Leonard and Alice Sayes made a statement to George Mountjoy, the executor of Harry's will, claiming that Beatrice had made no secret of the fact that she was poisoning Harry and had gloried in her deception of the police. She had asked them not to tell what they knew in return for half the insurance money and half what she would make out of selling her story to the newspapers. When Leonard had asked for his money she had offered him a derisory £20. Mountjoy tried to sell the story to the press, but instead the documents were turned over to the police. None of this was evidence against Beatrice, who in any case could not be tried again, though there was a curious passage in a letter she had written to the Sayes while in prison in

King's Head Hotel, Coleford. (Author's collection)

which she had said, 'I will be yours as ever I have been only do as I say. <u>Keep your tongue</u> quiet.' The main thing wrong with Sayes's story was that he described Beatrice poisoning Harry with powdered sheep dip mixed in the butter of his sandwiches. This was clearly impossible, as no trace of sulphur had been found in the body. Initially Sayes had claimed that he did not care what happened to him as long as he 'showed up that bitch', but when the police confronted him he realised that he was in danger of being prosecuted for libel. He said that if challenged he would say it was all a 'journalistic stunt'. With some regret the police decided that the case was too thin to proceed with.

Did Beatrice murder her husband? She had more than enough motive and every opportunity. It is clear from the expert evidence that Harry could not have absorbed a fatal dose though his skin, and even if this were possible he had not dipped any sheep since July, so this could not have accounted for his illness in December. If Harry had been well enough during his final illness to get out of bed and poison himself with sheep dip, which was a matter for some dispute, there would have been traces of sulphur in his body, but there were none. Also, as the coroner argued, a person who wants to commit suicide does not poison himself with small, repeated doses which cause great pain and suffering. That is a scenario for murder. The bottle of sheep dip solution remains a mystery. One possibility is that Beatrice had prepared it and added the potassium permanganate so Harry could use it as a mouthwash, which was a common use for it at that time.

As Dorothy admitted, life was more peaceful when her father was unable to get out of bed. Beatrice may have hoped that after his brush with death in July Harry would be less abusive, but the threat to kill his family on Christmas Day showed that a recovering Harry Pace was reverting to his old, violent ways. She must have feared that he would one day murder them all. Beatrice probably did poison Harry, but by doing so she may well have saved the lives of both herself and her children.

9

THE TORSO IN
THE RIVER

Tirley and Cheltenham, 1938

In 1938 there was only one crossing point over the Severn between Gloucester and Tewkesbury, and that was Haw Bridge, about half a mile from Tirley. Built in 1825, it consisted of a series of lofty iron arches resting on stone piles and carried the main Tewkesbury to Ledbury road, which was flanked on either side by stout iron railings.

The area was rarely busy in the small hours of the morning, which was why lorry driver Charles Hancock made a special note of some unusual behaviour on the bridge at 3 a.m. on 10 January 1938. As he was crossing the bridge on his way to Cheltenham a car had approached from the opposite direction, travelling at about 15 mph with sidelights on and headlights dazzlingly full. Hancock had dipped his lights several times, but to his annoyance the driver of the other car did not respond, and he had leaned out of his cab to shout angrily as the car passed him. The number plate was too dirty to read properly, and all he could make out was the curve of the top of the first letter, which meant it was either a P, D or B. The car was, he thought, a dark Austin Tourer, driven by a clean-shaven man wearing a dark overcoat and a trilby hat, with a similarly dressed man beside him. Both appeared to be aged between 35 and 40. In the rear seat was a bulky, shapeless object. His suspicions aroused, Hancock stopped his lorry at the end of the bridge and looked back. The car was now halfway across the bridge and had stopped by the footway on the north side. The two men emerged and looked around as if checking that the coast was clear. Hancock drove on, but the incident was still fresh in his memory when he picked up his newspaper on the morning of 11 January. That evening he went to the police.

About four hours after Hancock's sighting two local men, Hubert Dudfield, a salmon fisherman of Tirley, and Henry Ball were walking across Haw Bridge when they saw a canvas shoe and a chamois glove, both soaked in the overnight rain, lying on the footway. Ball examined the articles, threw them back where they had lain and walked on. Gradually it grew lighter, and about half an hour later Hubert Price, a roadman, crossed the bridge on his way to work. He too saw the shoe and the glove and was examining them when Ernest Clayton, a Tirley man, approached on his bicycle. Stopping to examine the finds, he saw what he was sure were bloodstains on the railings, both on the horizontal rail and the vertical iron supports. On the path lay what seemed to be fragments of flesh. Price removed the shoe and glove. He pondered the matter until lunchtime, then decided to contact the police. Samples of blood, the shoe, the glove, a small piece of bloodstained cloth and a scrap of flesh with tiny bone splinters were taken to Gloucester Royal Infirmary to be examined by pathologist Dr Davey.

On the afternoon of 11 January the police returned to Haw Bridge and found further items that may or may not have had something to with the mystery: a piece of red braid with a loop in the centre, a brown button with some strands of purple fabric attached and a woman's tweed belt made of similar fabric. By now the area was buzzing with the discovery, the main theories being that the remains were either those of a dead dog or sheep or a human hit-and-run victim. The only significant clue was a laundry mark on the glove, which was published in the newspaper, but no one could identify it.

By Wednesday 12 January, however, all the excitement was over. Dr Davey had examined the scant remains and said that, in his opinion, the blood was not human. The police announced that no further enquiries would be made.

It was 8 a.m. on the morning of Thursday 3 February when fishermen Hubert Dudfield and John Bevan placed their net across the Severn downstream from

Sydney Church and Hubert Dudfield trawl the river for remains. (Contemporary photograph)

Haw Bridge. They had a hut at a landing place about a mile from the bridge, and here they drew in the net to examine that morning's catch. What they found was so unpleasant that one of the men was at once sick. It was the torso of a man, swollen and putrefying, a piece of humanity from which arms, legs and head had been roughly removed. Tied around it were two pieces of twine, one under the armpits and one around the waist. To each of these, attached by lengths of cord, was tied a brick.

The police were soon on the scene, and the torso was taken to Cheltenham Hospital. There it was observed that while one arm had been removed effectively, the other seemed to have been roughly taken off with an axe. The legs had also been hacked off, and the head removed close to the body, in the hollow of the neck. Although it later transpired that there were no saw-marks on the body, the newspapers dubbed the discovery 'The Mystery of the Sawn-up Man'. By the afternoon it had been decided to call in Scotland Yard and engage the services of the most renowned pathologist of the day, Sir Bernard Spilsbury. On 5 February Scotland Yard and Gloucester police reviewed the case and went to Haw Bridge to survey the scene, with the intention of deciding whether the bloodstains found on 10 January were in any way connected with the torso. Eager crowds that had gathered on the river bank and also lined the bridge itself had to be ordered away.

There were three questions engaging everyone's mind: who was the victim? Was this a case of murder? And where was the rest of the body? Police with drag-hooks and divers arrived at the river and local fishermen were called in to assist. A 'bosun's chair' was roughly assembled from wood and rope, and in it Sergeant Shewry of the Yard was dangled precariously over the edge of the bridge so he could scrape up bloodstains, some of which were still visible on the railings. It was three hours before a drag-hook pulled up a right arm with a brick tied to it. Unfortunately the hand had been chopped off. Spilsbury arrived that evening, spent three hours examining the remains and departed with a number of specimens of flesh and fluids. He commented only that the torso was that of a well-nourished middle-aged man.

On 6 February the search went on, extending along the river, and newspapers estimated that about 5,000 spectators crowded both the river bank and the bridge. On the morning of 8 February a right leg was found about 250 yards from the bridge, and about two hours later the other leg was discovered. Both were weighted with a brick. The bricks attached to the body and limbs were all of the same kind. They were not new, but appeared to have been taken from a building and had traces of creeper.

In the meantime the police had been making enquiries about missing middle-aged men and by 6 February had made an interesting discovery. On the evening of 4 January Captain William Bernard Butt, aged 55, had left his home in Cheltenham without saying where he was going and had not been seen since. His absence had not been reported as he often departed abruptly and sometimes spent several weeks away. Captain Butt's wife suffered from a mental illness and required a live-in nurse, Irene Sullivan, whose only son, Brian, had been found dead – an

Sergeant Shewry scrapes bloodstains from the bridge, 5 February 1938. (Cheltenham Police Archives)

Crowds gather to watch the search for body parts, 6 February 1938. (Cheltenham Police Archives)

apparent suicide – on 24 January. From that moment the enquiry began to spawn a multitude of questions, most of which remain unanswered today.

William Butt was the son of a Worcestershire farmer. On leaving school he joined the army and spent many years in South Africa. He returned to England in 1909 and briefly went to live with his married sister, Gertrude Prew, at Aston-on-Carrant, but was soon in London looking for a suitable wife, motivated more by money than love. In 1913 he married Lillian King, a well-to-do widow. By 1915 he had rejoined the army and did not return to civilian life until 1919. He seems not to have suffered any wounds during his army life, although it is known that while serving in India he was hospitalised for syphilis.

Captain Butt managed a flourishing farm purchased with his wife's money but gave this up following her death from a heart attack in 1926. Returning to Aston-on-Carrant, he renewed an earlier acquaintanceship with Miss Edith Hogg. Miss Hogg was 46 years old, dumpy and plain, and known to be of a fragile mental state. She had every qualification Captain Butt required in a wife – she was rich. Captain Butt and Miss Hogg were married only five months after the death of his first wife. The couple lived at the large, rambling Manor House in Aston-on-Carrant for eight years and then moved to Cheltenham, where they rented a house at 248 Old Bath Road. Miss Hogg's properties, the Manor House and Manor Farm, were let.

By then it had become apparent that Mrs Butt needed constant care. Shortly before the move to Cheltenham Captain Butt had engaged Irene Sullivan to look after her. Three days after the new nurse's arrival, and much to her displeasure, the Captain departed without warning, going on holiday for a fortnight. These unexplained jaunts were to become a feature of the Butts' married life. Usually the Captain did not say where he was going, but sometimes he mentioned Oxford or Plymouth, and it was known that he had female friends in those places. The longest time he was absent from home was a period of six weeks.

When he was home he either ignored his wife or treated her with contempt. Sometimes he bullied her into signing over money to him, but in August 1934 he was granted power of attorney over her

Captain William Bernard Butt. (Cheltenham Police Archives)

Brian Sullivan with his dancing partner.
(Contemporary photograph)

property. Although the Captain had plenty of money to spend on himself and his lady friends he was otherwise mean with funds, and Nurse Sullivan had great difficulty in getting her £1 a week wages from him.

Irene Sullivan had been born Sarah Elizabeth Emma Fribbins in 1881 and married John William Sullivan in 1904. She later changed her first name to Irene. There were two children: Violet Eileen, born in 1906, who died of tuberculosis in 1925, and a son, Brian Johnstone, born in November 1909. By 1910 John Sullivan had gone – dead, according to his wife at the time, but she later admitted he had left her. Having to manage the best she could with no skills or qualifications, Irene Sullivan had become a private nurse, looking after elderly patients. Brian, with ambitions to be a professional dancer, went to London at the age of 21, became a dance hall host and started calling himself Byron Smith. Young Byron soon became popular with the clientèle at the Piccadilly Hotel. He was not, to judge by his photographs, a particularly handsome young man. About 5ft 7in in height, he was slightly built, weighing only about 8st 6lb, with a toothy grin, horn-rimmed spectacles, an incipiently receding hairline and an effeminate walk. Although a male employee of the hotel stated that Brian was a sentimental young man who often spoke lovingly of his mother, the dance hostesses said he could be mean and spiteful, sometimes pinching and twisting the flesh of their arms. According to his mother, he was highly strung and nervous in disposition, and friends confirmed that he was extremely squeamish, having a horror of blood. The idea of his killing someone and cutting up the body was, to those who knew him, ridiculous. The question of Brian's sexual orientation was later of some significance. Friends confirmed that he was interested in the opposite sex, and he was known to go on holidays with attractive girls. After his death several women claimed to have had romantic episodes with him. Rumours, however, suggested that he was homosexual. At no time did any male acquaintance report even a failed sexual approach. It is a subject on which much has been said, but nothing has ever been proved.

Brian lived in Flat 2 Radlett Place, St John's Wood in north London, which he shared with Keith Harold Newman, whom he had met at the hotel. Another friend was Brian Sutherland. Both of these young men were petty criminals. In 1933 Newman was sentenced to nine months with hard labour for obtaining goods by deception, and in 1934 Sutherland received a similar sentence for passing forged cheques. Before those dates Sullivan had started motor-hire businesses with the two men, both of which failed, and his mother had to bail him out financially. Despite this, Sullivan and Newman remained friends, and after extending the lease to Flats 2 and 4, Newman became Brian's tenant.

The building that later became of central importance in the deaths of Captain Butt and Brian Sullivan was Tower Lodge, Leckhampton Hill, Cheltenham, a distinctive two-storey house of ivy-clad grey stone with a castellated roof. Irene Sullivan, who was extremely fond of the property, first rented it in September 1933 and lived there for a year. Brian would drive down after work on Saturday night and spend the weekend with her. In 1934, needing finances, she sub-let it for another year, but after that it was largely unoccupied until July 1937. Conveniently the Lodge was only 10 minutes' walk from the Butts' home. Captain Butt also admired the Lodge and took over the rental in 1935. He was a frequent visitor and used the garden to grow vegetables. Occasionally Nurse Sullivan would go there with Mrs Butt. The only drawback was a lack of privacy. There was no front garden and no hallway. The front door opened directly into the living room and its low windows meant passers-by could look right in. For this reason, Brian had the front windows boarded up from the inside.

In the spring of 1936 Irene Sullivan noticed that Brian looked ill and worried, though he denied that anything was wrong. It was not until some months later that she discovered that two major changes had taken place in his life. On 1 February that year he had been fired from his job at the Piccadilly, after having been discovered thieving cash from the pockets of a wealthy customer, and on 5 April he had married Margaret Edwards, a businesswoman six years his senior. The couple had moved into Flat 2 Radlett Place, with Keith Newman as their neighbour in Flat 4. The marriage was unhappy from the start, as it became apparent that Brian was content to live off his bride, and they were finally to part on 4 January 1937. During this period Brian regularly visited Cheltenham to see his mother, often accompanied by young women. It was later rumoured that Brian was involved in criminal activities, perhaps transporting women who required an abortion, but no proof of this was ever forthcoming. His only known business activities related to property. In February 1937 he leased two cottages in Polperro and started to earn rent by letting them out in the summer.

In December 1937 Brian returned to Cheltenham to spend Christmas with his mother. During this time he slept at Tower Lodge but spent a great deal of time at 248 Old Bath Road, the Butts' home. The Captain and Mrs Butt spent Christmas and New Year with Mrs Prew at Aston-on-Carrant, arriving home on the afternoon of 3 January 1938. No one went out that night. Brian, as was his custom, visited his mother that evening, then went out for a drink at the

Wheatsheaf Public House over the road, returning briefly to say goodnight.

The following afternoon Nurse Sullivan went to the Lodge, where she saw Brian, who was happily relaxing with a book. When she returned at 5 p.m. Captain Butt abruptly ordered her to take his wife to the cinema but refused to drive them there. The two women left at 6.30 p.m., and were heading for the bus stop when Brian came by in his car and gave them a lift. They emerged from the cinema at 10 p.m. and took the bus home, pausing to chat to Brian, who again happened to be passing in his car. At no. 248 the ladies found the side gates and garage doors open. Captain Butt had gone again.

Over the next few days Brian called on his mother nearly every day, often popping in and out several times, and he always seemed in good spirits. He mentioned that on Saturday 8 January he planned to go to London to stay with Keith Newman, but that morning Newman sent him a telegram (neither Keith nor the Lodge had a telephone) saying he would be away at the weekend and asking Brian to come up on Tuesday the 11th instead.

According to Nurse Sullivan (and hers is the only account of Brian's movements during this critical time), on 9 January Brian went to no. 248 to have Sunday lunch, after which he took his mother out for a drive and a walk. He was full of plans for his Polperro cottages. On the way back he suggested going into Tower Lodge to have tea, but Mrs Sullivan wanted to get back to Mrs Butt, who was alone. All three had tea at no. 248, after which Brian went to the Wheatsheaf to have his drink, taking with him his dog, Bimbo, an elderly, black-and-grey spaniel of which he was very fond. He returned to say goodnight between 9 and 10 p.m. before going back to Tower Lodge.

Brian was back at no. 248 after lunch the following day. He was on foot: the car had not been taxed, since he was thinking of selling it. He left earlier than usual, at 9 p.m., saying he had an early start the next day, as he was going up to London. He promised his mother that he would telephone her and write when he got there. That was the last time she saw him alive.

Nurse Sullivan 'tells all' in the Empire News. (Cheltenham Police Archives)

At first, Nurse Sullivan was not too worried when she heard nothing from Brian. Neither, in view of his habitual absences, was she worried about Captain Butt. On the evening of 12 January she decided to pop up the road and have a look at the Lodge. She saw Brian's car in the driveway; to her surprise, Bimbo was inside it, barking, and the door was unlocked. The front door of the house was locked, as was the side gate, just as Brian would leave them when he went away. He always left a key for his mother under a stone in the drive, but this time it was not there. Unable to fathom what was going on she took Bimbo back with her to no. 248. She thought Bimbo could not have been in the car very long, as there was no mess and the dog was not ravenously hungry.

Nurse Sullivan had not been the first person to notice the dog in the car. On the morning of 12 January the milkman arrived to make his normal delivery (despite his stated intention to go away Brian had failed to cancel the milk and the newspapers), found the previous day's bottle still on the doorstep and saw the car in the driveway with the dog inside. He worried about it all day and in fact returned later that evening, but by then Mrs Sullivan had taken the dog away. On 13 January the previous days' deliveries were still on the doorstep, so the milkman decided not to leave any more. That afternoon, however, he saw that the milk had gone. In the meantime, daily deliveries of newspapers continued. On 14 January the delivery boy saw that the previous two days' newspapers were still sticking out of the letter box. No more were delivered.

Nurse Sullivan was by now becoming concerned. She returned twice more between 10 and 23 January (she was later unable to recall the precise dates). It was either 17 or 18 January when she saw newspapers blocking the letter box; she removed them and put them in the car. She was carrying a stick, which she used to tap on the side window of the house. All was silent. On the afternoon of 24 January she asked Mrs Butt to accompany her on the walk to the Lodge. This time, determined to get in, she took a screwdriver. The house was locked, as before, but there was one surprise: the window she had previously tapped on with her stick was open. Peering into the front room, she could see that the key which Brian usually left out for her was in the lock. She unscrewed the staples holding the padlock on the garden gate and found the back door open. Mrs Butt remained in the garden as Nurse Sullivan, now fearing the worst, rushed up the stairs, calling out for her son.

Brian was in bed. He was wearing pyjamas and socks, and the covers were drawn up to his chest. He lay partly on his right side, and blood had oozed from his mouth on to the bedclothes. His face was dark and his body cold to the touch. It was immediately obvious that he was dead and had been so for some time.

Nurse Sullivan touched the lock of hair that always fell over her son's forehead when he was sleeping, then she ran to the window and flung it open, gulping air. Rushing outside again, the sight of the plump figure of Mrs Butt in the garden was a jolt of reality. She decided to get her unstable charge home without alarming her. There, confused and unsure of what to do, she telephoned the one man she knew would have all the answers – her solicitor, Mr Thompson. Thompson at once contacted the police and then drove PC Llewellyn Merry to Tower Lodge, collecting Nurse Sullivan on the way.

Merry saw that in the bedroom part of the linoleum covering the floor had been turned back and a floorboard had been torn up, exposing a length of gas pipe which had been severed. All ventilation had been blocked with clothing and brown paper. There was a faint smell of gas in the room. He also found a handwritten note beside the bed. When he showed it to Nurse Sullivan she agreed it was in Brian's handwriting. Just inside the front door stood a pint bottle of milk, and in the sitting room was another bottle, part used. One item that excited no comment at the time was a slip of paper found in a wallet in Brian's suit. It was a receipt from Regent Motors for a Daimler motor car. Merry also found in the driveway part of a return railway ticket from Cheltenham to Gloucester dated 15 January. At Nurse Sullivan's request Thompson took charge of Brian's briefcase and his dog, Bimbo. There was no detailed search of the property. Nurse Sullivan, overcome by grief, went to stay with friends for a few days, while Mrs Butt had to be sent to a nursing home.

At the inquest, which took place at Cheltenham on 28 January, the note found beside the bed was read out. It read:

Please help my Darling mother, who has always done her best for me. I have not supported her as I should have done. I leave everything I possess to her absolutely, except my clothes, which I bequeath to K. Newman.

Much later Nurse Sullivan declared that this was not at all the sort of note Brian would have written. She began to wonder if she had been mistaken about the handwriting. And why, she asked herself, would he leave his clothes to Newman? Even Newman was puzzled by this.

The inquest found that Brian had taken his own life, but the coroner was unable to fix the time of death. Brian Sullivan was buried under a cypress tree at St Peter's church in Leckhampton Lane.

A week later, when the torso thought to be Captain Butt's was dragged from the River Severn, the police decided to search Tower Lodge. One of the first things they noticed was evidence of recent building work. On the bathroom wall was a patch about 4.5 x 2ft of fresh cement, filling a gap from which bricks had been removed. This was opened up but nothing unusual was found. The bricks, however, did have a resemblance to those tied around the body parts found in the Severn. The passageway carpet had been disturbed, and once this was removed loose boards were found which seemed to be a replacement for the bricks that had once made up the floor. The boards were taken up, and underneath was a hole, some 50in long, 18in wide and 18in deep. In it was a man's tweed overcoat, later identified by his sister as Captain Butt's. Nearby, in an alcove under the stairs, there was further evidence of brick flooring being taken up and of disturbed earth, but nothing suspicious was found there.

February 17, 1938. THE ILLUSTRATED POLICE NEWS & SPORTING RECORD 9

SPECIAL SKETCHES OF THE TORSO MYSTERY (SEE PAGE 2)

JAN. 4 CAPTAIN BUTT LEFT HIS CAR AT A GARAGE.

JAN 10. BLOOD FOUND ON HAW BRIDGE.

JAN 24 BRIAN SULLIVAN FOUND GASSED.

TOWER LODGE. NEAR CHELTENHAM. WHERE BRIAN SULLIVAN WAS FOUND DEAD.

FEB 3. FISHERMEN DISCOVERED THE SAWN-UP BODY OF A MAN IN THE SEVERN

FEB 6. DIVING OPERATIONS WATCHED BY 5.000 PEOPLE.

HUMAN LEG FOUND BY A BOATMAN.

POLICE SEARCH THE HOUSE OF CAPTAIN BUTT IN OLD BATH ROAD.

AN OVERCOAT FOUND SIX FEET BELOW THE FLOOR IN TOWER LODGE.

POLICE DISCOVERED WET PLASTER IN HOLE LEADING TO THE BATHROOM.

Sketches from the Illustrated Police News. (Illustrated Police News, February 1938)

In the garden shed the police found twine and cord very like those used to tie the bricks to the body parts. A pile of ashes in the garden was evidence of a substantial blaze, and there had also been a large fire in the living-room grate. When the ashes were sifted a great deal of partly burned male clothing was found. There were also a number of empty beer bottles and two four-bottle crates, which suggested that more than one person had been engaged in social drinking. The bottles had been supplied by the manufacturer to a local shop on 4 January. Brian was known at the shop, but it was not believed he had bought the crates. A number of plates were in a rack above the kitchen sink, and since Brian habitually used and washed one plate at a time this again suggested multiple visitors. Between the rafters and the roof was found a hatchet, which was sent for examination.

In Brian's bedroom there was a keyring with nine keys, one of which had been issued to Captain Butt, and a suitcase, once the property of the Captain's deceased brother-in-law, which the Captain was known to have used, containing some of Butt's clothing and personal items such as dentifrice and a razor, just the kind of articles he would have packed if he had been going away for the weekend. Also in the case was clothing belonging to Brian.

The Captain's Daimler was discovered at Regent Motors, Cheltenham. The attendant, George Griffiths, told the police that a middle-aged man had brought the car to him at about 10.40 p.m. on 4 January, and asked to garage it there for about three nights. A receipt had been prepared in triplicate, one part of which

The grave of Brian Sullivan. (Contemporary photograph)

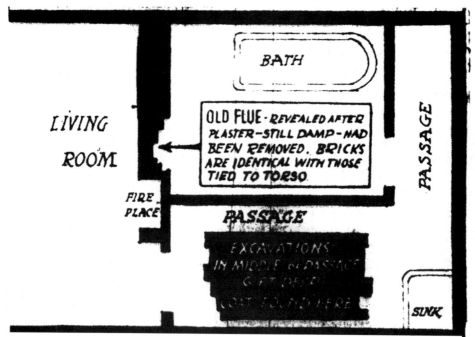

Plan of the ground floor of Tower Lodge. (Richard Whittington-Egan, *The Great British Torso Mystery*)

Sketch of excavations in the ground floor of Tower Lodge. (Richard Whittington-Egan, *The Great British Torso Mystery*)

Police officers and helpers dig the garden of Tower Lodge in the search for clues. (Cheltenham Police Archives)

was held at the office, one put on the car and the top copy handed to Butt. The log book of the car was later found in Brian Sullivan's case, and its ignition key in Brian's waistcoat pocket. The motor receipt, found in Brian's wallet, is the only piece of evidence that unequivocally connects the Captain to the Lodge at a point in time after he was last seen alive. The detailed examination of Tower Lodge having ended, eminent pathologist Dr Roche Lynch stated that in his opinion the dismemberment of the body had not taken place there. Brian's car was also examined, and nothing suspicious was found.

The laundry mark on the man's glove found on the bridge on 10 January was traced to Celia Greally of Piccadilly, a young woman with twenty-eight convictions for prostitution, who had married Keith Newman in 1931. They had been separated for two years but he still visited her, and Brian Sullivan was also known to be a visitor. Celia said that if a gentleman had left his gloves behind at her flat, they could well have been laundered before being returned to him. Newman denied that the glove was his, and its ownership was never determined.

On 8 February the police questioned Keith Newman. They asked him to provide an alibi for the period from 1 to 10 January. Two witnesses (including Mrs Margaret Frost, who had taken over 4 Radlett Place) said they had seen him in London every day during that time. Newman was not questioned further, and when he later issued a statement he tried as far as possible to play down any suggestion that he and Brian had been close friends. Later the fingerprints found at Tower Lodge and on the steering wheel of the car were compared with those of known criminals, including Newman, but drew a blank.

The torso was buried on 10 February at Cheltenham Graveyard, Bouncers Lane, Prestbury. The remaining limbs were buried on 2 May. The body was by then complete apart from head and hands, as the left arm had been found in the river on 19 February. Sir Bernard Spilsbury was in no doubt that the limbs belonged to the torso, and a pair of Captain Butt's shoes fitted the feet perfectly. He believed that dismemberment had been carried out shortly after death, before putrefaction had set in. There was bruising on the lower part of the back and both legs, which had taken place shortly before death. These were not the kind of bruises that would have been caused by striking with a blunt instrument but suggested either a car accident or a heavy fall. The condition of the remains was such that they could have been in the river since 10 January. It was impossible to determine cause of death.

The police now had to examine numerous statements in which people tried to recall, some four weeks after the event, the last time they had seen Brian alive, or the date on which they had seen activity around the Lodge. On the morning of either 6 or 7 January a witness passing by the Lodge had heard raised voices arguing, and thought that one was male and one female. On the evening of either 6th or 7th another passer-by claimed to have seen the front door open, a light on inside and two cars in the drive, while a man placed a heavy object in one of the cars. On the afternoon of 9 January two women were passing the Lodge when they noticed an unpleasant smell which they described as like someone burning the remains of their Christmas dinner. Another witness claimed she had smelled gas when passing the Lodge on 19 January.

Two policemen patrolling Cheltenham High Street. (Author's collection)

Someone had certainly been in the Lodge on 14 January. That afternoon John Bubb, an assistant of Shill's the local drapers, had delivered a package there. It was addressed to Nurse Sullivan, who had an account at the shop. The parcel was a package of sanitary towels, and it was marked 'urgent'. Unfortunately none of Shill's assistants could later recall who had ordered the item, although they were sure it was not Nurse Sullivan. When Bubb knocked on the door he heard a dog barking inside and a man's voice telling it to be quiet. Bimbo, it should be recalled, was then with Nurse Sullivan. The man who opened the door was about 30, clean-shaven, pasty-faced and with horn-rimmed glasses. He seemed agitated, grabbed the parcel and took it in. Bubb, who did not know Brian, was later shown his photograph but could not positively say he was the man.

A friend of Brian's said he had seen him in a public house, on either 5 or 12 January, when he had been agitated and unshaven, and had talked of making a trip to Gloucester. Was the ticket found in the driveway Brian's? A young man answering Brian's description had made the journey at about that time, but the ticket collector was unable to pinpoint the date. A Mrs Mustoe, who had started her new job as a cleaner on 17 January (which fixed the date in her mind), was walking past the Lodge on that day and saw a car outside. One man was already in the car; another got in and they drove away. The second man wore a coat of a kind Brian was known to wear. As a result of these sightings it was widely believed that Brian could have been alive as late as 15 to 17 January.

The police were also anxious to trace the car seen by Mr Hancock. The one that seemed to fit the bill best was the Austin Tourer once owned by Brian but which he had sold the previous November. In January 1938 it was owned by a builder who used it to transport paints and other materials in the back. It was garaged in an open stall to which anyone could have had access. Brian himself had once suggested borrowing it when his new car, the Austin saloon, was being repaired. The car was examined, but there were no traces of blood.

Trying to piece together a possible sequence of events from these fragmentary and sometimes contradictory and suspect observations was a difficult task. Colourful and fanciful rumours were rife, that Brian and the Captain had a homosexual affair, that Brian and his mother were involved in an abortion racket, that the Captain was involved in black magic rites, that Brian was part of a spy ring – and the wilder the accusations, the better the public liked them. There was no evidence to support any of these things. Indeed Nurse Sullivan later successfully sued Associated Newspapers Ltd on two counts of libel and received £1,000 in compensation. The answers to real-life mysteries, as opposed to works of fiction, are usually prosaic and simple, and it should also be pointed out that, had Brian been involved in an abortion racket, his finances would not have been at the low ebb they were at the time of his death. Not that money worries were potentially a reason for suicide, as his letters show he knew he could borrow from his mother. Nurse Sullivan may not have been a wealthy woman, but she did have some funds, small legacies from grateful patients.

The following account of events that January is speculation based on the known facts. Some time on 9 or 10 January, Captain Butt called in at the Lodge. Perhaps he interrupted Brian and/or some friends of his in criminal activities, and this led to his murder. Despite police conclusions that the body was not dismembered in the Lodge, it remains the most obvious place for this to have taken place. Dead bodies do not bleed, but they do leak fluids. Maybe the dismembering was done on a thick rug. A bloodstained rug was later found in the area but not officially connected to the case, and Brian is also known to have owned a tarpaulin. The large hole under the floor at the Lodge may have been considered a potential burial site, but this was evidently abandoned. Maybe it was felt that the odour of putrefaction would be too obvious – in the end only the coat was buried there. Some attempt may then have been made to burn body parts, but not for the first time a murderer would have discovered that human bodies do not burn that easily. Passers-by noticed an unpleasant smell. Other bloodstained items could have been burned in the garden. Plan C was disposal in the river. On 9 January, according to Nurse Sullivan, Brian was with her for most of that day, and the murder and dismemberment may well have happened during this time. That afternoon Brian suggested to his mother they pop into the Lodge for afternoon tea. He would hardly have done so if he had known that in the Lodge furious attempts were being made to dispose of a body. That evening Brian returned to a nightmare and became involved. No one wanted to use his own car, so Brian 'borrowed' his old one. On 10 January Brian's friends departed.

There is another slightly different scenario – that Nurse Sullivan's account of the events of 9 January are untrue, devised to protect the memory of her son, that Brian was present at the murder, was obliged to help his friends and may even have engaged his mother's help.

It was hinted many times in the press that the body found on 24 January was not Brian's, but his mother never doubted it. Remarks she made at the graveside that it was not her son in the grave were misconstrued, and she later stated that all she had meant was that the grave held only his mortal remains. It has also been suggested that Brian's death was murder staged to look like suicide, and that was certainly his mother's firmly stated belief, but there is no evidence of this. There were a few reported sightings of Brian after 11 January by people who knew him personally, but in all cases these were recalled weeks after the event, and there is nothing to precisely pinpoint the date. If he was alive after that date and in Cheltenham why did he not contact either his mother or Keith Newman? If he was in London why did no one see him there, and why did he not telephone or write to his mother? Why did he put Bimbo in the car and then apparently go away for several days? A great deal that was mysterious becomes clear if we simply assume that Brian died on 11 January.

That day Brian still planned to visit Newman, but then everything changed. The morning newspaper told him of the finds at Haw Bridge, and even printed the laundry mark on the glove. If the glove was Brian's then he would have known it was only a matter of time before enquiries led to his door. Psychologically, the time

The coroner, J.D. Lane, and Chief Inspector Worth attend the inquest on the torso. (Cheltenham Police Archives)

for Brian to have committed suicide was the night of 11 January or the following morning. He did not want to set the elderly Bimbo loose in the street or have him in the house where he might not be found for days, so he put him in the car, knowing that he would be found by someone in the morning, as indeed he was. One day later the newspapers announced that the remains at Haw Bridge had been declared non-human. Brian was off the hook – but by then he was already dead.

Brian's friends (who may or may not have been the same ones who had been there a few days previously) came to the Lodge on 13 January, took in the milk and placed the order at Shill's. If it was the same group they would have now felt safe, knowing that the police enquiries into the finds at the Bridge had ceased. Since the upper bedroom door was closed they may not have discovered Brian's body immediately, and quickly departed when they did.

The inquest on the torso that opened on 8 February was adjourned to 29 March. No cause of death could be determined, and on 5 April the jury finally brought in an open verdict on an unknown man. The torso has never been officially identified as that of Captain Butt.

Nurse Sullivan, adamant that her son was innocent of any wrongdoing and convinced that he had been murdered, moved to London. She died in 1945. The case disappeared from the newspapers, but there was a tragic echo twenty years later. On 20 December 1958, after heavy rain, the Severn was running fast and some 15 feet higher than usual. Navigation was hard, especially for the heavy fuel tanker *Darleydale H*, skippered by 40-year-old Stan Edwards. He successfully nosed it through an arch of Haw Bridge, but, caught by the current, the stern suddenly swung around and collided with one of the main piers. In seconds, the whole of the iron structure collapsed into the river, showering debris on to the barge's wheel-house. Edwards was killed instantly.

Nurse Sullivan attends the torso inquest. (Contemporary photograph)

In 1994 David Gladstone of Cheltenham claimed he had found William Butt's skull in 1978. He had been digging in the garden of his home at 22 Evesham Rd – an address where neither Nurse Sullivan nor Brian had lived – and uncovered a human skull wrapped in oilcloth. The skull, which appeared to have been soaked in acid, disintegrated as the police tried to lift it out. To add fuel to the claim, Gladstone said that in his cellar he had found furniture, including a bloodstained table, which he believed had come from Tower Lodge, and solicitor's letters addressed to Nurse Sullivan. None of these items could be produced.

The Haw Bridge mystery is unsolved. Nearly seventy years later we have no real answers – only questions.

10
STRANGE PRACTICES

Henleaze, Bristol, 1946–7

Cecil and Ann Cornock seemed like such an ordinary, respectable married couple, yet in the spring of 1947 the newspaper-reading public were to be regaled with stories of bizarrely erotic scenes being played out in their home at 142 Wellington Hill West, Henleaze, in the north-west suburbs of Bristol.

Ann Cornock was born Rosina Ann Keeling in 1912. Her father ran a small business as a painter and decorator, and the family lived in a drab but spotlessly kept home in a quiet back street of Bath. Ann was the eighth child of a marriage that produced one son and seven more daughters. She attended St Stephen's school not far from her home but did not sparkle academically. After leaving school at 14 she became apprenticed to a dressmaker in Bath and was there for four years. She then went into domestic service for two years. A sociable girl, she loved smart clothes and dancing. Her skill with the needle and her love of glamour must have brought a hint of style to the dance floor.

According to her parents, Ann's childhood ambition was to be a nurse, and she found a place in a hospital at Epsom as a probationer but was there for only three months, as the low wages were scarcely enough to buy the medical books she needed. She then became a nurse-attendant to the elderly. Disliking the long hours of night duty, this career too she abandoned, and in the summer of 1932, her dreams of becoming a nurse at an end, Ann went back into domestic service as a cook. After the tragic events of December 1947 Ann's experience as a nurse became of some importance. Enquiries were made, but no hospital in Epsom had any record of her as an employee. Claims that she had worked for six months at a mental home in Box, Wiltshire, could not be checked, as the establishment had closed.

On Boxing Day 1933 Ann Keeling attended a dance and there met her future husband, apprentice engineer Cecil George Cornock. Just a few months older than she, the tall, pale, angularly built young man must have seemed appealingly shy, while he, in what was clearly an attraction of opposites, warmed to her more forthright nature.

Seven months after their first meeting the couple were married at St Andrew's Church, Bath. It was not, Ann later claimed, a love match. She had married for the sake of security and a home of her own. That home was initially a flat in Bath. Later the couple moved to Uxbridge before settling at Kingswood, Bristol, living in a bungalow on Forest Road. A son, Maurice, was born in 1936. Cecil's career was progressing, and by the time the family moved to Wellington Hill West in 1941 he had a responsible post with the Bristol Aeroplane Company. He was a special constable during the war and was a familiar sight to neighbours as he set out on duty, his uniform noticeably overlarge on his slender frame. In 1943 another step up the career ladder brought him the post of cost inspector with the Ministry of Aircraft Production. His new responsibilities frequently took him away from home for long periods of time, principally to London, where he used take a room in a boarding house near Hyde Park.

Outwardly the Cornocks appeared to be a devoted couple, but if (as it later seemed) something was very wrong with the marriage, it may well have been the kind of partnership in which ill-assorted husbands and wives muddle along together to the end of their natural lives. Ann sometimes complained that her husband was mean and inconsiderate, and it was not long before she discovered another more unusual side to his nature – a taste for dressing in women's clothing and an addiction to pleasurable pain. In the twenty-first century a little cross-dressing and light masochism would not make the blood run cold, but in the 1930s and '40s it was regarded as a sickening perversion amounting to cruelty. Ann would have had no problem in obtaining a divorce on the grounds of her husband's behaviour, yet she remained with him, almost certainly for financial reasons. The only person with whom she ever discussed their unusual sex life was her sister, Mrs Hill, who on learning that Cecil liked to dress in women's clothing said, 'How ridiculous!'

Cecil's family saw the unhappy relationship from quite another angle. They later said that the couple rowed a great deal, and that Ann treated Cecil with contempt. She would demand money for clothes, and if he said he didn't have any she would become unpleasant, and had once smacked his face. She also

Cecil Cornock, Gilbert Kenneth Bedford and Rosina Ann Cornock. (Bristol Evening Post)

undermined him in front of Maurice, whom she would tell to take no notice of what his father said. Ann never mentioned an unusual sex life to Cecil's family, though she had told his sister that he had once put on women's knickers as a joke.

An unstable situation will explode only if a catalyst arrives to provoke the reaction, and in this case the catalyst took the unlikely form of Gilbert Kenneth Bedford. Born in Bath in 1922, he lived at 3 Midford Road and worked as a clerk. In 1932 he had contracted blood poisoning as a result of a swimming accident and spent several years in hospital. He remained severely disabled with a form of arthritis, his hip joints permanently fixed. In the street he walked with the aid of two sticks, though at home he was able to move about by supporting himself on furniture. On 5 August 1946 Bedford had gone out for the evening with his sweetheart, 21-year-old Pauline Keeling, Ann's niece. On the way home the girl had suddenly collapsed. She was admitted to hospital but died a few hours later from pulmonary oedema of unknown cause. The funeral gathering was at the home of Ann's parents, 6 Northampton Street, Bath, and it was here that Ann met Gilbert Bedford (usually called Ken) for the first time. At the time of their meeting Bedford was on the sick list with an ulcerated leg. He had been offered some treatment that required regular changes of dressings, something that he said his mother was too unwell to do for him. Ann offered to help, and that led to his visiting her in Bristol. Soon these visits became a regular occurrence. Some were short, but at other times he stayed overnight or for the weekend. Sometimes he slept on a settee in the front lounge, at others in the front bedroom normally occupied by Maurice, who was then moved to another room. Cecil appeared to be tolerating Bedford's presence, but he confided to his mother that the young man was spending a great deal of time at the house and he didn't like it. He intended to write him a letter telling him to keep away. He was also making plans to move to London and take Ann with him.

Cecil, who was frequently away from home during the week, cannot have known for sure how far things had progressed emotionally between his wife and their visitor. Letters passed between Bedford and Ann in which it was clear that they were on terms of great affection. They would kiss and cuddle, though Bedford's disability prevented anything more intimate. Ann told Bedford that she was not happy in her marriage, claiming that Cecil kept her short of necessities and bullied Maurice. She then confided a shocking secret. Her husband, she said, made her do terrible things and would not give her money unless she complied. These dreadful scenes often occurred in the breakfast room, and if Bedford should ever hear strange sounds coming from there he should go into the cupboard under the stairs, where a window gave a view through a glass-fronted cabinet, and he would see what she meant.

On the evening of Friday 6 December Bedford, Ann and Cecil were together in the lounge at 142 Wellington Hill West and Maurice had been put to bed when, according to Bedford's later statement, Cecil asked his wife to come into the next room and play draughts. She complied, leaving their visitor alone in the lounge. About an hour later curious noises started to emerge from the breakfast room,

The Cornocks' landing, along which the body was dragged. (From J.D. Casswell, *A Lance For Liberty*)

like the 'swishing of a stick'. Bedford, as directed, crept into the cupboard and peered through the window. Ann, he found, had not exaggerated. A portable washing boiler had been moved into the breakfast room and Cecil was leaning over it, tied hand and foot. He was wearing a dress, which was padded at the bust, and there was a gag in his mouth. Ann was beating her husband with a cane and saying, 'This is perfectly ridiculous; you must promise never to do this again,' to which Cecil's muffled response was, 'Lower.' After this incident Cecil retired to bed and the clothes were put away in a suitcase. Bedford now had no doubts about the ordeals Ann had to suffer which, he told her, made him feel 'quite sick'. It was wicked, he said, Cecil's making her do such things. She replied that sometimes it was worse. Sometimes they would go out into the woods and she would tie him to a tree and do the same thing.

At 1 a.m. on the morning of Sunday 8 December 1946 a telephone message was received by the St John Ambulance Association asking for an ambulance to go to 142 Wellington Hill West. It arrived seven minutes later, and Ann was standing at the door, looking calm and controlled. She told Mr Giles, the attendant, that her husband had decided to take a late bath. She had been talking to their friend Mr Bedford, and it was not until 11 p.m. that she had thought that Cecil had been in the bath a long time. When she went to check she found him with his head under the water, and they had moved the body into the bedroom. Giles found Cecil lying wrapped in a sheet on the bedroom floor, naked, and at once commenced artificial respiration. The police and a doctor were sent for, and

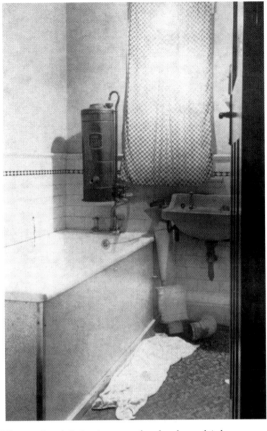

The Cornocks' bathroom, showing the broken flue-pipe. (From J.D. Casswell, *A Lance For Liberty*)

soon PC Buckland and Detective Sergeant Ivor Godden arrived. Godden checked over the bathroom. The bath was empty and dry, but there were traces of grit in the bottom, and the flue of the gas geyser used to heat the water was broken and lying on the floor in two parts. The window was closed and the curtains drawn. On the bathroom shelf was a child's wooden toy boat, an item that was later to achieve some significance. A denture was lying in the washbasin. Godden asked why the flue was on the floor, and Ann explained that it was broken off during the efforts to get Cecil out of the bath. When Dr Fells arrived at 2 a.m. he found resuscitation efforts continuing but quickly pronounced life extinct. He thought that death had occurred at least four hours previously. He noticed injuries on the body, which Ann explained as due either to the fall of the flue or to the clumsy removal of the body from the bath to the bedroom.

PC Buckland took a detailed statement from Ann, from which it appeared that the possible drowning of her husband had not produced that sense of urgency one might have anticipated in a loving wife. Cecil, she said, had had a cold and wanted a bath followed by a hot drink. She had run the bath for him, and just then there was a knock on the front door: Bedford had arrived. Cecil greeted him and afterwards went into the bathroom. This was about 10.30 p.m. Ann said that she and Bedford talked in the front lounge for a time, and then, realising that Cecil had not called out for his drink, she went upstairs and found him lying in the bath with his face under the water. Her first reaction was to take his pulse. Then she let the water out of the bath, turned off the pilot jet and called to Bedford for help. Together they tried to get Cecil out of the bath, a difficult task in view of the young man's disability. The first few times they tried the body kept slipping back into the water, and as Bedford steadied himself by holding on to the geyser flue, it broke away. Finally they managed to get the body on to the side of the bath, but before they could prevent it, it rolled on to the floor, the head striking the side of the door. They then dragged the body along the landing into the bedroom, where Ann said she removed Cecil's denture and applied artificial respiration, but without success. She was later to admit that despite her nursing experience she had never given artificial respiration before, though she had read about it. Faint and tired from her efforts, Ann then drank a cup of tea that Bedford had made for her and took two aspirins before deciding to go out to the telephone kiosk to telephone for an ambulance. Before help arrived she had spotted that the bath was dirty and gave it a quick clean.

After she had signed the statement the police officers noticed a damp jumper and skirt in the lounge. 'Have you changed your clothes this evening?' she was asked. She said she had, just before she went out to call the ambulance. 'A rather extraordinary thing, seeing your husband was ill,' said the officer. 'I didn't want to go out in damp clothes,' she replied.

Bedford's first statement to the police confirmed that he had arrived at about 10.15 p.m., and that at 11 p.m. Ann had gone up to the bathroom and called for him to come up quickly and help her. How quickly he was able to get up the stairs he did not say, but when he arrived in the bathroom, which was filled with Dettol™-scented vapour, Cecil's head was still under the water. Ann had neither pulled out the plug nor tried to support her husband's head. He helped Ann get Cecil out of the bath, during which efforts the geyser had been pulled down. Then, according to Bedford, they had turned him on his face in the bathroom, and Ann performed artificial respiration. Bedford said he then went and made some tea, as they were both upset, and they sat quietly in the lounge for a while. When Ann said she felt better they decided to take the body into the front bedroom. He estimated that getting Cecil out of the bath took about 20 minutes, and it then took them an hour to drag him the short distance into the bedroom.

Later, Bedford made a second statement in which he said, contrary to his first statement, that there had not been enough room in the bathroom for artificial respiration, and that this had been done in the bedroom, and that this was before, and not after, the tea had been made. This change of story was never explained, but the most probable explanation was the realisation that he needed to square his story with Ann's, in which resuscitation was attempted in the bedroom.

At 5.20 a.m. Detective Superintendent Carter arrived and took another statement from Ann, in which she said that soon after their marriage she discovered that her husband was a sexual pervert. Quiet, timid Cecil, it appeared, used to get angry and even violent if she did not comply with his wishes, and she had not had normal sexual relations with him for some years. The suitcase was produced and was found to contain a blue frock, ladies' underwear and some silk stockings. Some of the articles were stained with blood and semen. (A later search of Cecil's Hyde Park rooms revealed a bag of women's clothing in similar condition.) Ann then went to a store cupboard in the scullery and produced a piece of bamboo cane. 'It used to be longer than this, but it broke once when I was using it,' she said.

Carter was already deeply suspicious, increasingly so when he saw that there were differences in the statements made by the two witnesses. Bedford had spoken of an affectionate relationship between himself and Ann, which she emphatically denied, saying he only stayed there because she was looking after his bad leg. Bedford had spoken of tender kissing and cuddling. Challenged, Ann allowed only that there had been a friendly peck. She was obliged to admit that one item in her previous statement was a lie, told at Bedford's request. The young man had not, as both had previously said, arrived just as her husband was going up to have his bath on Saturday night, but had been in the house all day.

At 5 a.m. pathologist Dr Fraser arrived to examine the body of Cecil Cornock and found an extraordinary pattern of abrasions. There were bruises on the head, the backs of both shoulders, the backs of both legs, the wrists, the small of the back, shins, knees and ankles. He formed the opinion that the bruises to the wrists had been caused by Cecil being tied up with rope. When Ann was asked to produce the rope with which she had bound her husband, she went to the scullery cupboard and produced a peg bag with three pieces of white rope. When it was pointed out to her that the ropes were wet, she said that Cecil had dropped them in the bath.

On the following day Bedford admitted to the police that he had lied about his arrival time because he didn't want people to think he was a regular visitor. He now revealed that when the body was lifted from the bath Cecil's hands had been tied behind him with cord. Ann had said, 'The bloody fool would have himself tied up', and cut the cord away with scissors. 'We had better not say anything about the cord,' she told Bedford, 'or they might think we did it.'

The post-mortem confirmed that Cecil Cornock had died of drowning, but several injuries on the top of his head were undoubtedly received while he was alive and conscious and had been enough to stun him. These were not, it was thought, consistent with the head accidentally striking a hard, flat surface, such as a door. One explanation of the bruises was that Cecil Cornock had had his hands tied behind his back while he lay in the bath, and his legs were then held or tied at the ankles while he struggled violently. He had been struck over the head about six times with a blunt instrument, the most likely looking object being the wooden toy boat.

On 10 December Ann Cornock was arrested and charged with the murder of her husband. On the following day Superintendent Carter returned to the house for a thorough search and discovered a sack of waste paper with a number of torn-up letters in the handwriting of Ann Cornock and Kenneth Bedford. The fragments were pieced together.

The case came before Bristol magistrates in January 1947, Ann arriving for the hearing wearing a fur coat. The letters found in the Cornock house were read out in court. One, written in Bedford's handwriting, said:

Dearest . . . you do make me jealous . . . but cannot take any risk of losing you . . . I realise more and more that I could not go on without you, my dearest. You belong to me, and that knowledge has given me happiness.

In Ann's handwriting, a letter to 'Ken' read:

> . . . there is only one thing I am living for, and that is the day when I can say you are really mine . . . .

The magistrates had no hesitation in committing Ann Cornock for trial at the Bristol Assizes on a charge of murdering her husband, and she was placed in Cardiff Gaol to await the hearing. Bristol Corporation, anticipating the likely outcome of the trial, requisitioned the empty house at Wellington Hill West for a homeless family. On 7 February a routine medical examination revealed that Ann Cornock was two months pregnant.

The trial opened on 4 March 1947 before Mr Justice Croom-Johnson. No charge was made against Bedford. His disability made it impossible for him to stoop or lift heavy weights, and it was therefore believed that he would not have had the physical capacity to commit the murder.

G.D. Roberts KC appeared for the Crown, and the leader for the defence was Mr J.D. Casswell KC, an outstanding barrister who knew that he had a difficult, though not impossible, task on his hands. The extraordinary thing that struck him about his client was her calm, dispassionate demeanour – he referred to her afterwards in his memoirs as 'Poker Face'. He attributed this to her habit of suppressing all emotions during the years of her strange marriage.

When Detective Superintendent Carter gave evidence he produced a pieced-together letter written by Ann. Casswell spotted that it was unfolded, showing no

sign that it had ever been placed in an envelope or a pocket. He later used this fact to advantage when Ann claimed in the witness box that she had written it as a joke after Bedford had teased her that a friendly note she had written to him was not much of a love letter. The letter had, she claimed, been immediately torn up.

Bedford, who, it had been suggested by the prosecution, was the possible father of Ann's unborn child, denied firmly in the witness box that the relationship between himself and Ann had ever been sexual and admitted that he was a virgin. As he was obliged to hobble into the witness box on two sticks, the evidence carried some weight. He said that it was at his request that Ann had told the police he was not there earlier in the day. Having been present at the collapse of Pauline Keeling, admitting that he

Mr J.D. Casswell KC in 1938. (From J.D. Casswell, A Lance For Liberty)

had been in the house all of the day on which another member of the family had met a sudden death made him feel somewhat awkward.

Crucial to the case were the marks found on Cecil's body. In the witness box Dr Fraser was unshaken from his belief that the abrasions on Cecil's head were caused before death. He was not amenable to Casswell's suggestion that Cecil, exhausted from his strange practices and suffering from a cold, might have fainted. A plaster head was submitted in evidence, with black patches showing the position of the bruises.

Casswell was able to show the court that the toy boat in the bathroom which was alleged to have caused the head injuries showed no signs at all of having been used in that way. The defence then produced Dr Charles Gibson, assistant physician to the casualty staff at Bath United Royal Hospital and an experienced police surgeon. Gibson had undertaken an unusual experiment. He had asked an assistant to tie him up with cotton cord. Then, a quarter of an hour later, the cord was removed and he sat in a hot bath for half an hour. The cord marks still showed. Casswell used this piece of evidence to suggest that Cecil might not have been tied up while in the bath, the suspicious marks being those remaining from an episode of voluntary tying-up earlier in the evening. Gibson also thought that the abrasions on the head were consistent with Ann's story. He would not go so far as to say that they were caused after death, but he said they could have been caused by bumps on a flat surface while the condition of the heart was feeble. This of course would mean that Cecil was still just alive when hauled from the bath.

Gibson did not explain how the rope had got wet. Ann's own statement (from which the police witness would not be shaken, despite Casswell's best efforts) was that she had said Cecil had dropped the rope in the bath. A simple test for traces of bath soap or Dettol on the rope might have settled the question, but it was not done.

Which of the medical men would the jury believe? Casswell was experienced enough to know that the simple fact that two medical experts were opposed in their views could be enough to produce a reasonable doubt.

Finally Ann entered the witness box. She had sat calmly in the dock throughout the trial, not even glancing at Bedford as he gave evidence. This lack of emotion might have told against her, but in her favour was her sensible, determined manner and clear, convincing voice. Her evidence showed that she had made some last-minute changes to her story, which, it has to be said, is rarely a sign of innocence. She said that Cecil had often fallen asleep in the bath and that he had recently complained of black-outs, something he had failed to mention to his own doctor, and which she had not mentioned in her previous statements. The only explanation she could offer of the astonishing delay between finding her husband's body and calling an ambulance was that she was confused and distressed, and it never occurred to her. She had not, of course, been too confused to clean the bath, turn out the pilot light and change her clothes. She had, however, shifted her estimate of the time when Cecil went up to take his bath to 11 p.m., thus reducing that embarrassing and inexplicable delay in summoning help.

The Honourable Mr Justice Croom-Johnson. (From J.D. Casswell, *A Lance For Liberty*)

Her manner under cross-examination was firm and defiant. She admitted that she had not loved her husband but that their relations had been perfectly friendly up to the time of his death. Tackled about the signed statement in which she had said she had not had sexual relations with her husband for several years, she replied that what she had actually meant was that they had rarely had intercourse. The last time she had had intercourse with her husband was about a fortnight before he died. At the time of her original statement she had not known she was pregnant.

Roberts, prosecuting, drew from her the astonishing description of the events immediately following her discovery of Cecil with his head under the water. Her very first reaction, she said, was to take his pulse, and she believed then that he was dead. 'Was your husband's head still under water?' demanded Mr Justice Croom-Johnson. 'Just under,' she replied.

Roberts asked if she had any experience of taking pulses during her time as a probationer nurse, and she admitted that she had none. Since the taking of a pulse is one of the first things a probationer nurse learns, it confirms that she was not in that position for very long. 'Were you competent to take a pulse?' persisted Roberts. 'I don't know an awful lot about it,' said Ann.

She said that her next action was to pull out the plug and turn off the pilot light. It was only then that she lifted Cecil's head out of the water and called out to Bedford for help. This evidence conflicted directly with Bedford's description of the scene as he arrived in the bathroom: according to him, Cecil's head was still submerged. They then moved Cecil into the bedroom where he could be laid on the floor to receive artificial respiration. Ann had decided to attempt this herself, despite having never done so before. 'I am very fond of swimming and I have read quite a lot about it,' she said.

She admitted that she had not sent for a doctor and it had never occurred to her to ask Bedford to get help. He seems to have spent most of the time standing helplessly by or making tea. During two hours neither of them suggested that he might have gone next door for help or to the telephone kiosk, which was less than 200 yards away.

Ann's explanation of the love letters to 'Ken' was desperately unconvincing. Her allusion to waiting for the day when he could really be hers was, she said, suggested to her by Bedford, who thought he was in love with her, though she did not return his feelings: 'I was convincing him that I could write a love letter.' Roberts quite reasonably asked how this could be any concern of Bedford's. Ann said she thought Bedford was jealous because she was in love with her husband. This was patently ridiculous. She had already admitted in court that she did not love Cecil, and if she had been, then she would hardly have written a love letter addressed to another man. Her denial that the words she had written were sincerely meant was probably the most truthful comment she made on that subject.

In his final address Casswell suggested to the court that the conflict in the evidence given by Ann Cornock was due to tiredness from lack of sleep and exhaustion at her efforts to resuscitate her husband, and drew the jury's attention to the disagreement of the two medical experts. Roberts may have been less successful in convincing the jury that the motive for murder was the passion that the expressionless woman in the dock felt for Ken Bedford.

With the plaster head on the desk in front of him, Croom-Johnson summed up the evidence, urging the jury to steel their hearts against any appeals to sympathy. 'This case is murder or nothing,' he said. 'There is no room for a verdict of manslaughter or anything else.' In weighing up the medical evidence, he pointed out that Dr Fraser had had an early opportunity of viewing the injuries, whereas Gibson's opinion was not based on an examination of the body. He asked the jury to take the model head with them and consider whether the marks were accidental or caused by deliberate violence.

The jury retired for an hour and a quarter before returning a verdict of not guilty.

Ann seemed not to react, remaining motionless in the dock. 'Discharge her,' ordered Croom-Johnson. There was a pause as the verdict started to sink in. 'I said discharge her!' he repeated loudly. Ann left the dock and the court amid handshakes and smiles. Bedford, who had been visibly affected by the verdict, was assisted from court by an ambulance man. It was a stunning victory for Casswell in what must have seemed from the start to be a hopeless case.

The next day Kenneth Bedford, his love for and confidence in Ann Cornock undented by events, hastened to the register office to give notice of their impending marriage. The notice was withdrawn almost immediately. 'It is ridiculous,' Ann told a reporter. 'I am not interested in him. My friendship with Bedford is finished.' She headed for an undisclosed destination on the south coast.

Assuming that Bedford was telling the truth about the remarkable scene he had witnessed in the breakfast room, it must have been deliberately staged by Ann, with Cecil being led to believe that some mutual pleasure might be gained by having his guest spy on the proceedings. Ann's purpose was to secure Bedford's total loyalty to her, by making him witness the ordeal she was forced to endure. After the trial Ann Cornock returned to Bath, where her daughter was born in the autumn of 1947. Neither she nor Bedford, who died in 1997 aged 75, provided any further enlightenment as to what happened on the night of 7 December 1946.

BIBLIOGRAPHY

1. THE CAMPDEN WONDER

Clark, Sir George (ed.) with chapters by The Late Viscount Maughan and Dr D. Russell Davis, *The Campden Wonder* (London, Oxford University Press, 1959)

Overbury, Sir Thomas the Younger, *A True and Perfect Account of the Examination, Confession, Tryal, Condemnation, and Execution of Joan Perry, and her two sons, John & Richard Perry, for the supposed murder of William Harrison, Gent. . . . Likewise Mr. Harrison's own account.* (London, Rowland Reynolds, 1676)

Rudder, Samuel, *A New History of Gloucestershire* (First published 1779; this edition Alan Sutton, Gloucestershire, 1986)

Rushen, Percy C., *A Handbook of Chipping Campden;* (Woodbridge, G Booth, 1905)

——, *The History and Antiquities of Chipping Campden in the county of Gloucester,* (London, published by the author, 1911)

Stephen, Leslie, (ed.), *The Dictionary of National Biography* (London, Smith, Elder, 1885–1903)

Tyus, Charles, *The Power of Witchcraft, being a most strange but true Relation of the most miraculous and wonderful deliverance of one Mr William Harrison, of Cambden [sic], in the county of Glocester [sic], Steward to the Lady Nowell [sic]* (London, Three Bibles on London Bridge, 1662)

——, *Truth brought to light* (London, Three Bibles on London Bridge, 1662)

Barnsley, Mr, letter to John Gough in an edition of Sir Thomas Overbury's pamphlet held by the Bodleian Library.

Wood, Anthony, notes written on an edition of Sir Thomas Overbury's pamphlet held by the Bodleian Library.

www.campdenwonder.plus.com

The International Genealogical Index – available in libraries on CD ROM and at www.familysearch.org

2. LEGACY OF DEATH

Anon., *The Bristol Fratricide: being an exact and impartial narrative of the horrid catastrophe of Sir J.D. Goodere, Bart. Perpetrated by the contrivance of his brother S. Goodere Esq.* (London, J. Hart, 1741)

Anon., *The genuine Dying Speeches of Capt. Samuel Goodere, Matthew Mahony and Charles White* (Bristol, B. Cole, 1741)

Anon., *The New Bristol Guide* (Bristol, R. Edwards, 1799)

Anon., *The Trials of Samuel Goodere esq.; Matthew Mahony, and Charles White, for the Murder of Sir John Dineley Goodere Bart* (London, A. Millar, 1741)

Anon., *The trials of Samuel Goodere, M. Mahony, and C. White, for the murder of Sir J.D. Goodere (brother to the said S. G.) on board his Majesty's ship, the Ruby: at the sessions held in Bristol* (London, H. Goreham, 1741)

Dodson, M., *The Life of Sir Michael Foster, Knt. Sometime one of the judges of the court of King's Bench and Recorder of Bristol* (London, J. Johnson and Co., 1811)

Foote, S., *The genuine memoirs of the life of Sir John Dinely [sic] Goodere, Bart.* (London, T. Cooper, 1741)

Latimer, J., *Annals of Bristol in the Eighteenth Century* (Bristol, J. Latimer, 1893)

Minchington, W., *The Port of Bristol in the Eighteenth Century* (Bristol, Bristol Historical Association, 1962)

Penrose, J., *The Reverend Mr Penrose's Account of the behaviour, confession, and last dying words of the Four Malefactors who were executed at St. Michael's Hill at Bristol, the 15th of April, 1741, viz. S. Goodere, M. Mahony, and C. White, for the murder of Sir J.D. Goodere, Bart., and J. Williams for the murder of her bastard child* (London, Eliz. Applebee, 1741)

Reid, W.N. and Hicks, W.E., *Leading events in the history of the port of Bristol* (Bristol, Western Daily Press, 1877?)

Smith, R., *The Fratricide, or the Murderer's Gibbet, being the right tragical Hystorie of Sir John D. Goodere, etc.* (Bristol, Bristol Mirror Office, 1839)

Wells, C., *A Short History of the port of Bristol* (Bristol, J.W. Arrowsmith, 1909)

Wilkinson, J.W., *The life and works of Samuel Foote* (Kent, unpublished typed copy, 1956) (British Library)

3. A SHOT IN THE DARK

Anon., *The Trial at Large of John Penny, William Penny, Thomas Collins, John Allen, Daniel Long, John Reeves, James Jenkins, Thomas Morgan, James Roach, Robert Groves and John Burley, for the Wilful Murder of W. Ingram . . . likewise the trial of W. A. Brodribb, gentleman, For administering an Unlawful Oath to the above persons* (Gloucester, D. Walker and Sons, 1816)

Dougall, John, *The Young Man's Best Companion and Guide to Useful Knowledge,* (London, Bungay, 1815)

Australian Churchman, June 1886

Cheltenham Chronicle and Gloucestershire Advertiser

Parish records of Berkeley, Hill, Stone and Thornbury

International Genealogical Index

4. REVELATIONS

Anon., *The National Gazetteer of Great Britain and Ireland* (London, Virtue and Co. 1868)

Tomlinson, Dr K.M., 'The Edmonds's Case, Newent's Victorian Murder?' *Transactions of the Bristol and Gloucestershire Archaeological Society,* vol. 113 (1995), 167–78

Newent Local History Society, *Chapters in Newent's History* (Newent, Newent Local History Society, 2003)

Gloucester Journal

Ross Gazette

Pall Mall Gazette

The Times

Records of births, marriages and deaths held by the Family Record Centre, London

5. TRIPLE EVENT

Anon., *The National Gazetteer of Great Britain and Ireland* (London, Virtue and Co., 1868)

Gloucester Journal

Gloucester Mercury

Gloucestershire Chronicle

Bristol Mercury

Bristol Daily Post
Clifton Chronicle
Records of births, marriages and deaths held by the Family Record Centre, London

6. VIRTUE AND SIN

Stroud Journal
Stroud News and Gloucestershire Advertiser
Gloucester Journal
Gloucestershire Chronicle
National Archives ASSI 6/28/4
Records of births, marriages and deaths held by the Family Record Centre, London

7. THE MAD CYCLIST

Anon., *The National Gazetteer of Great Britain and Ireland* (London, Virtue and Co.,
    1868)
Rudkin, Revd Messing, *History of Horsley* (Dursley, Whitmore and Son, 1884)
Gloucestershire Chronicle
Gloucestershire Echo
Stroud Journal
Stroud News and Gloucester County Advertiser
Records of births, marriages and deaths held by the Family Record Centre, London

8. THE POISONING OF HARRY PACE

Herbert, N.M. (ed.), *A History of the County of Gloucester* (London, Victoria County
    History, 1996)
Hyde, H. Montgomery, *Norman Birkett: the Life of Lord Birkett of Ulverston* (London,
    The Reprint Society by arrangement with Hamish Hamilton Ltd, 1965)
Dean Forest Guardian
Gloucestershire Chronicle
The Times
National Archives, ASSI 6/63/2, MEPO 3/1638
Records of births marriages and deaths held by the Family Record Centre, London

9. THE TORSO IN THE RIVER

Whittington-Egan, Richard, *The Great British Torso Mystery* (Liverpool, The Bluecoat
    Press, 2002)
Cheltenham Chronicle
Gloucestershire Echo
Daily Mail
Daily Mirror
The Times
Records of births, marriages and deaths held by the Family Record Centre, London

10. STRANGE PRACTICES

Casswell, J.D., *A Lance for Liberty* (London, George G. Harrap and Co. Ltd, 1961)
Bristol Evening Post
Bristol Evening World
The National Archives, DPP 2/1570
Records of births, marriages and deaths held by the Family Record Centre, London

INDEX